5
12

Editorial

THE MEMOIRS
OF GENERAL DELGADO

General Humberto Delgado greets his supporters as he arrives at a polling
station in Lisbon to vote during the 1958 elections

The Memoirs
of
General Delgado

CASSELL · LONDON

CASSELL & COMPANY LTD
35 Red Lion Square · London, W.C.1
and at
MELBOURNE · SYDNEY · TORONTO
JOHANNESBURG · CAPE TOWN · AUCKLAND

———

© Opera Mundi 1964
First Published 1964

Made and Printed in Great Britain by
C. Tinling & Co. Ltd., Liverpool, London and Prescot
F.164

CONTENTS

v

CONTENTS

PART FOUR

ILLUSTRATIONS

PREFACE

On 28th May 1926, the general dissatisfaction felt by all Portuguese political parties except the one actually in power, impelled the Army to intervene in face of the breakdown of the political life of the nation. A show of strength sufficed to oust the Government without the slightest violence.

In 1928, Dr Salazar, who had taken no part in the revolution, was appointed Minister of Finance and, in 1932, Prime Minister. I have had to work with him on military affairs during the Second World War and later in connection with civil aviation and therefore I knew him quite well. Thus I am in a position to give an historical account based on first-hand experience.

While still merely Minister of Finance during his first years of power, Dr Salazar earned a justifiable reputation for having brought some form of order into his particular sphere. He had achieved this by eliminating the long-standing deficit, reducing the National Debt, prohibiting all expenditure which could not be met by receipts and by revaluing and stabilizing the currency.

Some of his enemies, who have allowed hatred to overcome their common sense, are scornful even of this period of Salazar's life and scoff at him for his unimaginative orthodoxy, but I uphold his drastic methods, although I was hard hit by the national recovery tax.

His mistake lay in continuing to apply these methods indiscriminately to a sick financial system and, once his promotion to Premier gave him full power, in extending them to every aspect of the nation's life which showed any lack of stability.

Once he was promoted from cold, impersonal duties in the Treasury to the long-term, vigorous task of planning the nation's future, he failed utterly and the outcome has been a wealthy, stable state founded upon poor, starving masses. By

ix

employing the restrictions of a totalitarian state, he has brought about a tragic standstill and at times a serious retrogression in the evolution of the Portuguese people especially in the political and cultural spheres. He has not been able to resist the age-old attraction of power, which has become the driving force in his life, for even longer than the thirty-five years he has ruled, his only love has been his cold-hearted devotion to study and his only passion his wish to govern. This became obvious during my electoral campaign in 1958, when I stood as Opposition candidate for the office of President of the Republic and, unlike the other opposition candidates who had all withdrawn on the eve of the elections, I showed Salazar that I intended to take my chance at the polls. At least I let the world see for the first time just what Portuguese elections are like. According to the press throughout the world, all that took place both before and during the elections was a farce, especially the incident on voting day, 8th June, when the Government, with shameless audacity, issued the infamous bulletin in which it prohibited Opposition observers from being present at the polls. One can only wonder why elections are held at all!

On the nights of 2/3rd June and 18/19th December 1958, the problem of Portugal was meant to be and should have been settled by armed revolutions which I was to command. Unfortunately the officers taking part refused at the last moment to go forward in this patriotic venture.

As a result of the first disciplinary action which Salazar brought against me after the elections, I was ignominiously discharged from the services on 7th January 1959. I therefore became a civilian and my only link with the Air Force was the derisory pay to which I have been reduced, and even this was stopped altogether after my second trial. After my thirty-six years of service they wanted to plunge me into destitution.

When I heard that P.I.D.E., the secret police, were planning to arrest or kill me, I was urged both by military and civilian friends not to let myself be seized. I therefore sought asylum in the Brazilian Embassy in Lisbon as I felt that there was not sufficient time to make the necessary arrangements for another revolt. I shall explain this in detail later.

During my ninety-eight days in asylum, my name appeared in newspapers throughout the world and this occasioned even more attacks from the dictator.

I arrived in Rio de Janeiro on 21st April 1959, which happened to be the Day of Tiradentes, the symbol of Brazil's independence, who was hanged as a rebel against Portuguese sovereignty. Coming to Brazil was bliss and it also gave me a good opportunity to bring out my political memoirs. A publisher soon presented himself and asked me to have the book ready in two months. I would have done so, were it not that certain indispensable personal documents were held in the Embassy in Lisbon and it took nearly a year to have them secretly forwarded to Brazil, in spite of the great efforts made by my good friend, Ambassador Álvaro Lins.

In the meantime, I gave the dictator no peace. I had promised the Portuguese people that the 'electoral campaign' was not over, for we were robbed of success and have the right and duty to go on fighting.

I have recently returned from a political mission to Venezuela, Britain and Holland, and in all these countries I rejoiced in freedom to attack the Portuguese government by speeches, through the press and on radio and television—admittedly, the Minister of Justice in Holland did hesitate for a few hours about television, but this was undoubtedly on account of pressure from Lisbon. In Britain all three main political parties received me.

I have paid dearly for criticizing Salazar, which, in his opinion, is a crime. He has had me discharged from the Air Force; I have lost my income, and have a family to maintain. I took a job as Chief Public Relations Officer in the firm 'Alimentos Selecionados Amaral S/A', of São Paulo which, it is interesting to note, is owned by a Brazilian, Rui Amaral Lemos. The Portuguese were afraid to employ me, no doubt lest the long arm of Salazar might reach them in Brazil.

In 1960, the excellent book by Álvaro Lins, *Mission in Portugal*, rocketed white-hot into the fight against the dictator.

In January 1961, the spectacular affair of the *Santa Maria* took place.

Encouraged by my example, several Portuguese have sought asylum in the Lisbon embassies, among them an Opposition group led by Manuel Serra, my fellow revolutionary and conspirator in Lisbon, which made its way to Brazil.

This combination of circumstances caused someone to suggest that the time was ripe for me to revive the idea of a book, intended as a factual record by one whose rightful place was in Belem Palace, instead of which he found himself in a food factory doing the equivalent of a lieutenant's work.

This memoir is an account by one who can offer quite a variety of experience, occasionally of some value; he knows the dictator well and holds no personal grudge against him; he has travelled widely over five continents and spent eight years in military and air diplomacy in free countries; he has helped to make democracy work at international conference tables; he has studied for nine years in universities and military academies, and he reveres the great Corsican's principle 'Let's fight the battle and leave the rest till afterwards'.

Maybe this is worth very little. The reader will decide for himself.

Humberto Delgado

PART ONE

CHAPTER I

How I grew up under the Monarchy and under the Republic

As I come to look back over half a century, I feel somewhat lost among the welter of tangled impressions which, as William James says, are engraved on millions upon millions of specific cells in the brain which, under threat of death, can spring to life. At such moments scenes from one's past flash by at a dizzy pace like a film—as I once experienced when the aeroplane that I was piloting, solo, stalled and crashed in flames.

I can recall with some clarity a number of impressions of my earliest childhood. I can see one scene which took place when I was four years of age: my father fashioned a flag out of paper, green and red, and sent me out on to the street with it, to cheer for the Republic among crowds of people wild with enthusiasm. That was on 5th October 1910, the day on which the Monarchy fell.

As far as politics are concerned, one could say that I fall into the classification of 'born republican'.

Usually, a republican was anti-clerical and made a point of declaring himself to be an atheist or an agnostic.

My father (and my dear friend), now dead, was an Army officer and a republican. On the other hand, my most indulgent mother, now over eighty years of age, was, and still is, a profoundly devout lady, rather superstitious, and with a veneration for the '*ancien régime*'. I was, as a consequence, rather like a football between the two of them. They both worshipped me, too. I was the only boy among their four children. I represented

3

as it were the '*grand seigneur*' who would one day raise the family prestige to new heights.

The hopes of my parents and of my sisters were all focused on me, in the sense that I gave the family the gloss that it lacked, due to some sort of spiritual weakness and to the diffidence which is inherent in those who are always in the rearguard of society or of their class. This was indeed the case. Never having gone through one of the higher military schools, my father became an officer very late in life—so late in fact that when he died on 29th April 1944, he held the same rank as I did, that of major, and if he had lived for a further two months he would have had me as his 'superior' officer with the rank of lieutenant-colonel. In short, he cherished a kind of grudge, a score to settle with the Army, where father and family were always at the end of the line. . . . His son, as 'a product of the Officer Training School'—tantamount to being an academic figure, would even matters out. The family, full of pride, would rejoice in his boy's triumph.

Because of this state of mind, I have felt ever since I was small that it was essential to get ahead of others. I admit, however, that this idea well suited my temperament which was abounding with pride and well-larded with vanity. To tell the truth, I did not need pushing, I already was pushing.

At five years of age, my father set me learning to read. At eight, very much ahead, I completed my primary schooling with distinction—something to which I became accustomed. Paradoxically, it is to this that I attribute the disadvantage all through my later life of always seeming to be the youngest in training or on duty. A disadvantage because, although I was poor and defenceless, I was always the constant target for malice and envy and even for bullying by ill-intentioned individuals older than I was but at the same stage in their studies as me. My country, Portugal, is small and poor, and the struggle for life there is harsh and exceedingly bitter.

On the other hand, the fact of starting my life in this way enabled me from a very early age to mix with older people, and this helped to bring me to a precocious maturity. Take as one example the following:

A vivid picture dances at the point of my pen. It was in

Torres Novas, a small town about a hundred kilometres north-east of Lisbon. When I was eight years old, Sô Paulo,[1] the big teacher in the fourth class in the primary school, told me to stand in for his colleague who taught the third class, when he was away from school. How wonderful it felt as I went up to the dais on which the teacher's desk stood and sat down in his chair! The Corsican Emperor cannot perhaps have felt quite so happy when he was crowned by the Pope. It was a great experience in human contact. Grown up for the moment, I corrected the reading lesson, taught children of my own age or even older than myself and talked to my teacher 'colleagues'. Teachers in the primary schools were practically all republicans in those days. From the clash of views between my father and my mother, I had absorbed from my mother the 'fear of God' and had developed my instincts of kindness and protectiveness towards the weak. From my father I learned to eschew the practice of religion. And, because of him, there grew up in me profound sympathies and convictions to complicate my life: a transcending love of justice and hatred of oppression. So much so that, going far beyond my father in this respect, I sometimes became terribly angry with him if I saw him doing anything unjust or tyrannical.

The female side of my family used to exhort me not to get into fights with the other boys, but I did, of course, and enjoyed it, sometimes getting home rather the worse for wear. My father urged me to manly deeds—even bull-fighting and trying to throw cows by their horns when I was ten years of age and very, very frightened.

In this way I gradually developed a keenly analytical mind, helped by my parents' divergent outlooks on life.

I was six years old when monarchist incursions took place in 1912; eight when German troops attacked Cuangar in Angola, although Portugal was then still neutral in the First World War; and ten in 1916, when Germany finally declared war on Portugal and my father left for France. My recollections

[1] *Sô.* Popular abbreviation of *Senhor*: Mister. (Translator)
[2] Monarchists in exile in Spain, led by Paiva Couceiro, crossed the border into Portugal hoping to attract popular support for a rising against the Republic. They were unsuccessful. (Translator)

of this latter period are more vivid and it might be of interest
to form them into the basis on which to present some important
historical events. The main interpretation naturally came from
my father's lips, with the crudity and sincerity of an ordinary,
unassuming man, always eager to study and acquire knowledge, but lacking a sound educational foundation.

The Reactionaries

The bitter anti-clericalism of the republicans has a definite
historical basis, arising out of the struggles of the liberals in the
nineteenth century.

The Sovereign Congress of 1821, in the absence of King D.
João VI, who had fled to Brazil, decreed the abolition of the
Inquisition—that institution whose memory the Church of
Rome has never, to my knowledge, publicly repudiated. The
authority of the ecclesiastical courts was also assailed. The
liberals made enemies at that time with whom they were to live
in a state of cold war right up to 1920, when peace was made
between them and the Republic.

On 29th March 1821, the day on which the oath of fealty to
the fundamentals of the monarchical constitution was to be
sworn, the whole of Lisbon was illuminated, bright with hope
and optimism. But the palace of the Papal Nuncio remained in
darkness, and this inflamed the Lisbon crowds who stoned and
smashed its windows. Always lagging behind, once again the
Church sought to cast a cloud over the sun of liberty.

The Church and the Armed Forces are the most conservative
and unchanging institutions in the world. The Church is
more so than the Forces, since in the latter those who do not
change their tactics accordingly tend to get killed off in
battle. . . .

Republican hostility has its roots in, and is nourished by,
the fact that the Church is to a large extent supported from the
Public Treasury, the priest being a special kind of civil servant.

As Oliveira Martins says, referring to the period following
the fall of the régime of the Marquis of Pombal, 'the weakness
caused by the Catholic delirium will turn the people into
imbeciles'. I was to confirm the truth of this during my election
campaign in 1958, half a century after the establishment of the

Republic. The majority of the priesthood then preached against me from the pulpit, in medieval terms: 'the anti-Christ who is coming'; 'Beelzebub who will burn down churches and shrines'! And all this, despite the religious tolerance which was a feature of my proclamation to the country, coming from someone who is considered to be what is known as a 'Catholic by tradition', whose daughters are former students of Catholic schools in Canada and the United States and who is married to a Catholic lady endowed with the highest classical virtues.

One can appreciate then how great priestly influence must have been in 1910, on a population living mainly in country districts, very largely illiterate and given to speaking of witches and werewolves as though they were living creatures as real as their cattle or pigs.

The whole thing needs to be set in its chronological context, for everything is relative.

Portugal began to live under a democratic system of government only fourteen years after the liberal insurrection of 1820, forty-five years after the French Revolution, and fifty-eight years after the Declaration of Independence.

However successful and creative the revolution, there can be no doubt as to the tremendously backward situation from which it arose. Nevertheless, it is well known how much the liberals succeeded in achieving in a short space of time and in a country where the mass of the people lived in ignorance and servitude. The whole atmosphere of the country was transformed and brought up-to-date. In particular, Mousinho da Silveira, the Minister of Justice and Finance, took the historic step of doing away with entails and Church benefices yielding less than 200 *milréis*, and of abolishing the practice of confiscation of property, slavery in the islands, tithes and sundry other survivals from medieval times.

A Royal Family with little to recommend it

Unfortunately, the Armed Forces' regrettable habit of taking a hand in politics began to take root with fatal results: unrest, and rebellions which from now on were to become commonplace.

The instability of governments became notorious. The

7

rebellions of 1836 and 1837 set the pattern, particularly the latter in which two marshals, Saldanha and Terceira, were embroiled. The constitutional jig began all over again with the best constitution being chosen from among those already in existence. From 17th April 1838 to 9th February 1842, five ministries followed one upon the other. One, the ministry of the Duke of Palmela, lasted only for a few days. The same sort of thing was to happen under the Republic in its final phase.

Because the majority of the nation had very little education, far less than the average in the Latin countries of Europe, the constitutional monarchy fell into the hands of D. João VI, a king devoid of any manly characteristics, a figure of fun to his people and the head of an abnormal family. The Queen, Carlotta Joaquina, for example, was the source of a great deal of scandal. She was a woman of absolutist and despotic inclination and savage instincts. In 1805 she conspired with a group of noblemen and tried to have her husband declared incompetent to rule. Because of this, she and the king decided to live apart. This decision gave rise to the allegation that D. Miguel—the absolutist—was not the King's son although he was born in 1802. It was he who began the practice of falsifying elections, using extraordinarily blatant methods which were later revived under the Salazarist régime. I shall have a word to say on this in due course and with ample evidence to back it up. In his letters sent out to the chambers which would elect the people's representatives, there appeared the contemptible suggestion *that they should choose delegates that were above suspicion of being liberals!* Passing on to D. Luiz, King from 1861 to 1889, one finds in him a figure curiously like a present-day liberal. As I saw in an old magazine which came to light in my parents' house, the King was even caricatured, wearing a nightcap and using the telephone, then just introduced. How inconceivable it is, seventy years later, that a caricature of Salazar cannot appear in any Portuguese newspaper!

In 1867 the death penalty was abolished and then slavery, in all the territories of the Portuguese Crown. It makes one shiver to see in Alfredo Pimenta's *History of Portugal*, which is approved by the Salazar government as 'the only textbook to be used in the state schools', the attempt to justify slavery as 'a magnificent instrument of colonization'.

The colonies

New ideas gained currency in the nineteenth century with regard to the rights of sovereignty in Africa. Our country, however, swift in the work of discovery, was not so in occupying new lands.

The Conference of Berlin in 1884–5, although called together on the initiative of Portugal, turned out to be inimical to her immediate interests. There is a popular saying: 'to go for wool and to come back shorn'.

Indeed, the conference made a number of decisions in the face of Portuguese opposition, relating to freedom of navigation on the Niger and Congo Rivers; it established freedom of navigation in the Congo basin; laid down the doctrine that sovereign possession of territory demands effective occupation of that territory; and created the Congo Free State as the 'private domain' of the King of the Belgians.

Significant factors seemed to conflict one with the other. On one hand, increasingly disregarded, were Portugal's 'historical rights'; and on the other, there was the extraordinary slackness and indifference of the monarchist governments. Administrative posts in the colonial service were awarded simply by favour, in order to help protégés get rich quickly. Britain sought her colonial governors from among civil servants with practical experience of administration and then made them serve five years in one post. In Mozambique twenty governors would come and go in the same space of time! The consequence was nothing but disorder.

Gungunhama, the Vatua King of Gazaland in Mozambique, refused to pay any tax and sought to negotiate a treaty with the Portuguese King. This colonial crisis was finally brought to an end in 1905, thanks to the energy and courage of Mousinho de Albuquerque. The politicians rewarded him, in the usual way, with calumny and intrigue. Suicide ended the life of this worthy officer, who was unready to adapt himself to the ways of unprincipled petty politicians.

Weakness in Africa reflected in more sombre colours the

9

ineptitude and folly which was rife in Portugal itself, where liberty was confused with licence, democracy with demagogy or anarchy (in the perjorative sense of the word), words with deeds and dreams with reality.

The Monarchy falls

The result of meddling in politics by marshals and military personnel generally was that it came to be considered quite normal that officers on the active list should have a hand in political affairs.

João Chagas, in his history of the Oporto Revolt, makes it clear that the Monarchy carried the spirit of tolerance to such lengths that for a long time it allowed to figure among the leaders of the republican party individuals who held high rank and responsibility in the Army. Liberty there was indeed, and more. . . . Latino Coelho and Souza Brandão were generals. José Elias Garcia was a colonel and a teacher at the Army School. A republican organization in Lisbon had as its secretaries an officer of the Navy, Nunes da Mata, and an Army officer, Homem Cristo. The latter was the greatest pamphleteer of the century, over forty years older than I was, and very much later on, when I was grown up, he was to favour me with his great friendship. He was already in his sixties when I was a young lieutenant. We would meet to preach morality in the demoralized Portugal of 1926. (His family told me that they had come across letters of mine in the large body of correspondence which he left when he died, over eighty years old, in 1943.) One trait I had in common with Homem Cristo: detestation of meaningless words, contempt for rhymes or slogans which affront one's intelligence, abhorrence of the search for a scapegoat. This latter vice goes a long way back. Under the Monarchy, during the ministry of Cabral, they used to sing:

'*Vão às eiras os pardais?*
De quem é a culpa senão dos Cabrais?'
(Are the sparrows going to the threshing floors?
Whose fault is it except that of Cabral's supporters?)

But it was the King who was the scapegoat for everything

bad that happened, despite the fact that his power of action was circumscribed by the Constitutional Charter.

When one looks through the newspapers of the period, what stands out clearly from all of them is that politics were based on personal abuse and on a fever to win power from sheer vain lust to wield power! One can see the indifference to the fundamental problems of a democracy which, if not an economic democracy, was at least a political one; the murky moral and physical corruption and decay were equally evident. At that time, instead of the stability enjoyed by Britain and other democracies in Europe which had reasonably long-lived governments, in Portugal ministers came and went like streaks of lightning. As we shall see later on, this was the case under the Republic as well as under the Monarchy.

D. Carlos acceded to the throne on 19th October 1899, in the thick of this atmosphere of corruption and civic apathy and ignorance. A month later, on 15th November 1899, Brazil proclaimed herself a Republic. This event breathed new life and heart into the opponents of the Monarchy.

In a country whose economic life was out of step with that of the rest of Europe and hag-ridden by parasitic classes, political parties became mere cliques of business associations and their clients. A job in the Civil Service was something that people dreamed about. 'It's pensionable, my son'—that was the refrain of mothers in a country where the working man, without insurance or financial aid in old age, dies in beggary or from starvation.

The monarchists, in a cretinous, cowardly state of hypnosis, paradoxically helped to create the myth that the root of the trouble lay in the King—who did not rule.

The political scene in Portugal was thoroughly chaotic and conditions were opportune for the British ultimatum of 11th January 1890, which demanded that we should no longer presume to consider as Portuguese territory vast tracts of land on the borders of Mozambique. Otherwise, relations with Portugal would be broken off in twenty-four hours.

Without seeking to mitigate or excuse the brutality of this ultimatum, the truth must be stated—that Britain, before delivering that tragic document, had thrice called attention to the critical situation in Africa, where two ambitions and two lines of imperial policy crossed one another and were in conflict. One was to link Luanda with Lourenço Marques, with Portuguese territory stretching right across the continent from east to west. Our old allies, on the other hand, planned to link the north and south of Africa, with British territory stretching from the Cape to Cairo. But the politicians and the whole of Portugal were steeped in the pettiness which Eça has described so pungently and wittily.

Portuguese patriotism did, however, reassert itself. The scapegoat was, nevertheless, once again the King! The Republican party gained strength but split, showing its usual weakness, into republicans in the strict sense of the term, democrats and federalists! Later it split even more. They were half a century away from having their cake and yet they were already dividing it. History repeats itself.

What with all the hot air, the attacks on the King, the corruption and the ultimatum, the contagion spread to the Armed Forces which became even more politically minded and undisciplined. Even sergeants were allowed to write for the newspapers and to run a newspaper of their own, which was distributed openly among the ranks and presented to the ministers responsible for the Forces!

The Republic came into being in this atmosphere of demagogy, indiscipline and senselessness. The first republican revolt broke out on 31st January 1891, while the country was still raging with indignation over the British ultimatum. It was a revolt confined to half a dozen officers of minor rank and to sergeants and was quickly suppressed. It was merely the sap rising.

The Monarchy lingered precariously on. As with Salazar today and even with the Opposition in Portugal, the myth arose of securing external aid, the panacea for all ailments, instead of using the only true remedy, an internal one.

Edward VII visited Portugal in 1903. D. Carlos reciprocated in 1905. There followed visits by the King of Spain, the Kaiser and President Loubet of France. . . . Everything seemed to be quiet. But in 1906 a revolt broke out in the Navy aboard the Cruisers *D. Carlos* and *Vasco da Gama*.

Brito Camacho very appositely wrote in *A Luta* (The Struggle) the following words which were to become famous: 'The more liberty they give us the more we must demand, compelling ourselves to compromises which degrade or to violent deeds which cannot be undone.'

In April 1907 the King called upon João Franco to assume office, and, a fatal step, agreed to the dissolution of parliament.

When the dictatorship published the decree which gave it wide powers to make life miserable for the republicans, the King was assassinated, on 1st February 1908. Both D. Carlos and the heir to the throne, D. Luiz Felipe, were killed.

That was the end. There followed the vacuum of the reign of the boy-king D. Manual II and then on 5th October 1910 the Republic was established by half a dozen disengaged junior officers, army sergeants and by the people. The monarchists, with only a few exceptions, looked on passively. Later, however, they were to hinder the progress of the Republic.

Our fair and lovely Portugal, the garden of Europe 'set on the shores of the sea', is a strange place. With all her faults I love her dearly. Feeling and logic are worlds apart!

CHAPTER II

The early days of the Republic

As care was not taken of some of the people who helped to establish the Portuguese Republic or who adhered to it from motives of greed or ambition, what could be the outcome of a régime born as this was amongst an illiterate people, who would go through a period of constitutional government paying greater attention to the verbal fireworks of the intellectuals than they did to the efficiency of their statesmen? It was difficult for things to go smoothly in a republic which was created by a few gallant junior officers, some of whom were mentally and intellectually rather limited. Young men are fine for breaking new ground. Afterwards no one knows what to do with them if they are ambitious.

Right through to 1913, internal agitation greatly hindered the progress of the régime. The monarchists who had failed to defend the Monarchy in 1910 now organized incursions from outside the country. This, indirectly, considerably swelled the numbers of defenders of the Republic who were later to invade the ministries with hands outstretched, trying to pick up jobs on the most diverse levels, many of them quite beyond their capabilities.

Up to 1912 my father was serving in the 8th Artillery. Although an auxiliary officer, he was selected to command an Artillery division against a possible monarchist invasion by way of Penamacor, a small village on the frontier in Beira-Baixa.

How proud I felt! The regimental commander went to fetch my mother and us children in the officers' mule cart.

Enthusiasm reigned in Abrantes, that quiet little town whose name a century earlier Napoleon had used when bestowing the title of duke on General Junot, who had commanded the French invasion of the Iberian Peninsula in 1807.

The mounted artillery of that period made a strange and colourful picture—a jumble of guns, mules, horses and swords. Although for four years I used to go round the barracks sampling the soldiers' rations with relish when my father was supplies officer for the day, I must confess that it was not until then that I was bitten by the determination to join the Army. I would be a soldier. And so, ten years later, off I went into the Army, against the advice of very many of my contemporaries who, though they had not done so well academically as I had, had gone into the more lucrative professions. To tell the truth, I had been greatly impressed by seeing my father when he first became an officer commanding a unit bound for active service. There he was at the head of his men, with his pistol in its black holster, the lanyard around his neck, and holding the reins taut lest his horse got too far ahead. This would not only have obliged the column to break into a trot both uncomfortable and tiring but was also forbidden.

The mounted column was really a tiny affair, consisting of two guns and their respective ammunition wagons, the field kitchen and not much else. Nevertheless, as each wagon had a futchel and was drawn by three pairs of mules, the little troop seemed like some sort of fabulous serpent, destructive and apocalyptic—to my young eyes.

The guns were the Schneider-Canet 7·5 cm. quick-firer, model 904, to use the official description. Without possessing the extraordinary efficiency of the '*soixante quinze*'—that elegant weapon of the French Artillery which was to amaze military experts in 1914–18 by its accuracy and range—nevertheless the Schneider-Canet, immaculate as it rumbled noisily through the streets, with the buglers sounding a military march, presented a magnificent spectacle.

As always, the population adored the regiment. They took pride in seeing the mules pulling away mightily, straining against their well-fitting harness. The drivers stirred their beasts to greater exertion by cracking their whips noisily. And so the mules mastered the steep hill which rises on the right bank of the Tagus. To me, it was all so thrilling. And the whole lot was commanded by my father. And he had been specially selected for command, not just there by virtue of seniority! I knew. I had heard other officers saying so.

The Republic at work

Fortunately, the terrible dead weight of professional orators and of revolutionaries who degenerated into dangerous, addle-brained fanatics or into troublesome malcontents did not prevent the emergence of Afonso Costa as a leading personality. A man of action, he gave the country a 'new look', in its legislation at least.

The Ministry of Justice, Costa's own ministry, published laws governing the civil registration of marriages, the separation of Church and State, leasehold, the press, the family, the defence of the Republic, and many more. It was a new world. From the Ministry of Labour came laws dealing with hours of work, a weekly rest day and the right to strike. In this connection it should be noted that under the Salazar régime the seven-day working week continues to exist in secret, for the many thousands of workers in grocery stores that have adjoining restaurants and bars. The latter stay open on Sundays and the staff are shunted to them from the stores.

The Ministry of Education, finally separated from the Ministry of the Interior, prepared far-reaching schemes of reform for the educational system. The Higher Technical Institute was established and various reforms were carried out to improve the schools.

It became optional to wear the medieval, unhygienic and expensive student uniform known as *capa e batina* (cloak and cassock). The archaic system of academic courts was done away with. Legislation for scholarships was introduced.

At last a Ministry of Colonies was set up, bringing to an end the anachronistic fusion of naval with colonial affairs. The old arrangement was perpetuated to a great extent, I think, because of the perquisites which it provided and, as a matter of tradition, still provides for naval officers who have become millionaires through their colonial appointments, and often have scarcely anything to recommend them except their white naval uniform.

The First Republic's Ministry of War began to reorganize the Army, intending to bring it up to date and to make it more democratic. To this day, half a century later, I can remember the words and tune of a song that my father taught me, and which was popularized among the soldiers in order to bring to an end the misuse of the national anthem which was prevalent in the period immediately after the fall of the Monarchy:

> '*É honra ser soldado da República,*
> *É honra defender a Liberdade.*
> *Soldados, avante! avante!*
> *Por essa vida fora . . .*'

> (It is an honour to be a soldier of the Republic,
> It is an honour to defend Liberty.
> Soldiers, forward! forward!
> For that life outside . . .')

I think it might be of interest to show the high moral principles which inspired some republicans. Not many people in Portugal are aware of what I shall now relate.

Through my father I learned of a confidential circular issued when the Republic was first set up, intended to bring to an end the humiliating and indiscriminate use of 'tu' as the normal term that officers and sergeants would employ when addressing soldiers in Portugal. (This is the way that most ladies speak to their servants.) In my country soldiers are always addressed by their number alone, like animals. Sometimes an ordinary sergeant, who may have struggled through his primary education while serving in the ranks, avails himself of the traditional right to address any recruit straightaway by his number, using 'tu', even though the recruit may have a cultural level vastly superior to his own.

As I was to confirm for myself throughout my life, the intention was not respected but, on the contrary, derided. It was, and still is, very noticeable how after fifty years have elapsed officers and sergeants use in speaking to soldiers not only 'tu' but expressions and gestures which range between contempt and obscenity. This has always struck me forcibly and I have had some serious disagreements over it with comrades-in-arms.

Splits in the ranks of the republicans

Even at the first meeting of the Republican party on 11th June 1911, the stubbornness and incompatibility of some of its members made themselves felt. The Republican party split into various groups: the largest of them—the 'republican' group—was called by the people at large *Democrats*, to distinguish its new position. This group was led by Afonso Costa. My father belonged to it since, in my view regrettably, the Republic had allowed officers on the active list to take part in politics. Another group, the *Gradualists*, was headed by Antonio José de Almeida and the third, the *Unionists*, by Dr Brito Camacho.

Paradoxically the P.R.P. (Partido Republicano Português), the most radical of them, was the one which absorbed most of the monarchists who adhered to the republican cause. I say 'paradoxically' but it may perhaps be the normal thing with 'amoeba-like' individuals.

When self-interest impels them to change, they do so with the maximum amount of noise! Some, very few, remained monarchists, holding perhaps to the rigid, stupid principle that the only honest man is the one who never changes his mind. Others, going to the opposite extreme, pragmatists and always in line with everything and everybody, adhered to the republican cause *en masse*. 'We are always on the side of the Government . . . Is it our fault if the Government changes?' . . .

The working class—illiterate, uneducated and anarchistic—rebelled against everything and everybody, causing disorder and unrest on any pretext whatsoever, in the absence of an organized socialist party which could formulate and put forward the legitimate demands of the underprivileged, intelligently and honestly.

The Democratic party was in the ascendancy until 1st January 1915, when it was overthrown by a military putsch.

The constant movement of troops, not bound for action against foreigners, which I saw as a child, remains a curiously vivid recollection. How confused it made me to see republican set against republican. . . .

To complicate life even more for a budding republican, the First World War broke out in August 1914. Lamentably, the Gradualists (divided amongst themselves), the Unionists (who were prepared to accept that the country should go to war provided it was only in the colonies!), the monarchists and the working class all chose this tragic moment to attack the Government, thereby hampering its war policies. It was a time of national disgrace, as neither was entry into the war prevented nor was participation willingly accepted. The syndicalists and the extremists led by Machado Santos, a naval officer who, in common with many others, was dedicated more to petty politics than to his profession, began to play in street affrays and disturbances the role that was imputed to the Democrats. Consumed by envy and malice, the republicans devitalized the régime and made it permanently ineffective and the scene of a savage struggle for the 'fruits' of power.

Things had reached the depths when, as a boy of ten, I was to hear officers and civilians sneering that 'Norton[1] and Afonso Costa had sold the soldiers to England at a pound apiece'!

I still remember the occasions when, as a student at the Military College, in the streets of Lisbon I used to run into civilians armed with Mauser-Vergueiro rifles (the Army type) and ordering people to stop or to turn aside. It struck me then —'What were the Army and the police for?' It also confused me. I would hardly say that I understood much better some years later and it disgusted me. When I used to query it, people would answer me evasively or by naming politicians —like gods or devils—who were at odds with one another.

The system falls apart; the clergy; women

Other factors contributed to the break-up of the new system, quite apart from the premature fragmentation of the Republican party.

The 1914–18 War, for example, broke out too soon for a

[1] Norton de Matos. (Translator)

19

republic that had only recently come into existence. Other inimical factors were clerical reaction, working-class demagogy, the dictatorial propensities of the Democratic party and the revolutionary aspirations of the monarchists who, led by Azevedo Coutinho, tried in 1913 once again to put the clock back.

The clergy, too, were enraged and resorted to violence in order to demonstrate their opposition to the abolition of religious oaths in the courts. They opposed in every way they could the suppression of the religious houses and of saints' days, the prohibition of religious instruction, and the introduction of the divorce law. The Government was obliged to forbid the reading of the relevant pastoral letter in the churches. Bitter controversy ensued. In my home, my father and my mother held different opinions. I was aware of this, but just did not understand.

Against this background of renovation and change there appeared in 1911 the first woman civil servant at the Board of Public Credit. Women were beginning to press their demands. Prominent in the feminist movement were Carolina Beatriz Angelo, a doctor, and the writer, Ana de Castro Osório. The latter was known to all children of my generation. Here was something new. The Republic held out a helping hand to the weaker sex. Naturally, my dear mother's generation looked askance at 'these women who go about the streets aping men, instead of staying at home mending their husband's socks' . . . !

On 25th January 1915, President Manuel de Arriaga invited General Pimenta de Castro—a man who stood aloof from political conflicts—to form a ministry. This was the 'conservative' reaction against the ascendancy of the Democratic party. But the 'man in the street' was by then too strong for a military putsch to be attempted. The Government lasted scarcely four months. I remember how terribly frightened my mother was by the bloody revolution of 14th May 1915 which restored the Democrats to power. Along with the General, naturally, fell the President of the Republic, Manuel de Arriaga.

On 9th November 1915, by the normal process of a demo-

cratic parliamentary majority, Afonso Costa became Prime
Minister.

The First World War and the reactionary régime of Sidónio Pais

On 10th March 1916, when the Government commandeered
the German ships anchored in the Tagus, Germany declared
war on us. The masks were torn off at last. In fact we had been
fighting German troops in Africa ever since 1914. The set-up
in small countries run by inexperienced politicians is sometimes rather like a comic opera.

On 15th May 1916, a coalition Government of 'Sacred
Union' was formed, with Antonio José de Almeida as Prime
Minister. Prominent in it were Afonso Costa, Minister of
Finance; Major Norton de Matos, Minister of War and
Augusto Soares, Minister of Foreign Affairs. The Unionist
party remained in opposition. It opposed the war! Short-lived,
this Ministry of Sacred Union fell in April 1917 after having
suppressed another attempt at an uprising by Machado Santos
on 13th December 1916. (Governments came and went so
quickly that it has become almost essential to give their dates
of existence in full, with months and days. . . .)

Right in the middle of the war—and against it, as the soldiers
at the front (including my father) well knew—an armed
coup d'état brought to power on 6th December 1917 Major
Sidónio Pais, formerly the Ambassador to Germany and
Professor of Mathematics at the University of Coimbra. The
reign followed of 'Sidónio's cadets'—a high old time for
Germanophiles, reactionaries and adolescents, some of whom
made a name for themselves before they had even come of age.
Some were to reappear under Salazar's dictatorship.

Thousands of miles away, the greatest revolution of all time
took place. In October 1917 the Bolsheviks seized power in
Russia. I remember clearly a newspaper interview with a
refugee woman who said that people were even eating corpses
there. I could never afterwards blot out from my mind and
from my senses the feeling of cold horror that I experienced
as a small boy when I read that news item.

Disorder and instability at home had their effect, too, at the
fighting front in Flanders. The energy of Norton de Matos had

sufficed to get the troops to France, but not to keep their morale as high as it should have been. My father, then in charge of ammunition supplies for the Portuguese Expeditionary Corps, told me that one night he had received an order to supply ammunition for possible use against a battalion, which, sick and tired of war, was seething with mutiny. He also told me that he had met a doctor who was carrying on clandestine propaganda against the war. . . . My father had warned him that he would give him a thrashing if he were again to find him engaged in this harmful activity.

On 6th November 1917, a month before the Sidónio Pais revolt, the Portuguese Expeditionary Corps became independent, lacking only aircraft and heavy artillery. When Sidónio Pais came to power, everything started to deteriorate. As my father, fighting in France, said, 'We see nobody over here any more and anyone who goes home never comes back again.' I heard people at that time say that they volunteered for war service but that they never got sent to France.

After ruling for less than a year, Sidónio Pais was assassinated on 18th December 1917. I was twelve years old at the time and was one of the party of school children who mounted a guard of honour over his coffin. At one point, apparently when a number of shots were heard, the crowd panicked. I was facing north towards the National Theatre situated in the Rossio, the principal square of Lisbon. The tremendous pressure threatened to overwhelm the coffin. Standing in the second row, I spontaneously 'about faced' and others followed suit. The War Ministry subsequently praised us collectively.

I learned a great lesson then when I was twelve—to be cautious when dealing with crowds. . . . They cheer and applaud but they also shove, and they will only refrain from trampling you down if they feel your bayonet tickling their tummy. . . .

The conservative ministry which followed under Admiral Canto e Castro led a very sorry life. One revolt followed another. The entire Armed Forces were dabbling in politics. The First Republic came into being like this and was to die like this. In 1919 a monarchist uprising broke out in the north which was to last from 10th January to 13th February. Then another uprising, a monarchist one as well, flared up in Lisbon at Monsanto on 22nd January. This resulted on 24th January in a republican victory and produced yet another crop of 'heroes' to be handsomely rewarded. Some entered the Military School at the same time as I did in 1922, despite the fact that vacancies were supposed that year to be reserved exclusively for ex-students of the Military College. By way of exception individuals were admitted who must, moreover, have been too young for them possibly to have been in action. ... My innocent mind found it all very strange.

And, along with some good ones, what a peculiar lot came into the Military School through the string-pulling of 'important people'! Very many of them never completed the course, although helped and favoured in every way by important personages in the Republican party.

As an eighteen-year-old cadet just starting adult life, I was already beginning to lose confidence in the Republic.

New elements began to exacerbate the disorder and confusion in which the nation found itself. Strikes became endemic between 1919 and 1924 and even affected the public services! In 1922, for example, while a cadet at the Military School, I worked in the Post Office during several brief stoppages. And most acceptable it was indeed to a penurious cadet to get extra pay for those days. But how I wondered at all the disorder that I saw around me! My final shock came when the 'Red Legion' spread terror everywhere, like vultures battening on the corpse of the Republic which had come into being so radiant with promise.

During the First World War I felt for my own part (my father being a lieutenant with four children) the dire effects of the sorry train of events—inflation, unstable prices, shortage of goods, the '*nouveaux riches*', the flight of capital, the revolutionary syndicalists, the harassment, and sometimes the pauperizing, of the middle class—for which the 'conservative' policies of Barros Queiroz in 1920 provided no solution. I was then fifteen years old. I remember events from then on much more clearly. I can 'relive' 19th October 1921, the occasion of a fresh revolutionary atrocity in the murder of the Prime

Minister, Dr António Granjo, whose life Cunha Leal tried heroically to save. Two naval officers and founders of the Republic, Machado Santos and Carlos Maia, were also assassinated. The name Cunha Leal was on everybody's lips. He was a man for whom I had a great respect and affection, even when I criticized him.

Our mothers, and women generally, began to dread the anarchy which had grown up under the Republic while I, little boy as I was, sometimes wondered what it all meant.

During this preliminary phase which preceded my first serious change of attitude politically speaking, with regard to the government of the Republic, three things impressed me which really shattered my naïvety and innocence.

When I had completed the course at the Military College, i.e. the high-school course, I enlisted as cadet-sergeant in the 8th Artillery at Abrantes. There I was going to stay, from August to October 1922 until the Military School began its new session, when I was to enter the course there after a medical examination and a few supplementary tests. It was distressing to see the state that the regiment was in. The officers showed up at eleven and some of them never stirred beyond a room where they amused themselves playing back-gammon and draughts.

At that age, I was naturally interested in horses. There were, however, practically none. One day—almost a red-letter day —a dozen arrived and I ran to see them. To my horror they had the letter R branded with a hot iron on their haunches and were beasts already worn out in the cavalry and rejected as unfit for further military service. Normally they would have been sold to gypsies and poor farmers. It made one's heart ache to see the way in which their bones seemed to stick right through their hides, the way their hair came out and all the other pitiful signs of neglect and overwork.

Months later I entered the Military School—now the Army School. One teacher there often frittered away his lecture periods in telling jokes instead of teaching ballistics and weapon-drill. The examination syllabus included the hand grenade but teaching how to use it correctly was neglected. On one occasion a live grenade exploded in class and it was only a matter of luck that the students were not killed. Most of them ran for their lives!

Finally, a teacher of history not greatly endowed with knowledge of his subject, instead of putting into the urn all the tokens for the dozen or so subjects which might fall to the students' lot in the examination, just put a few of them in. In this way he had less to do and his students succeeded in making a better showing. . . .

There is a story that on one occasion a student pretended to read out the number on a token which he had drawn from the urn. Making a tremendous '*faux pas*', the teacher fell right into the trap and called out, 'Impossible, that one is not there'. The burst of laughter which followed reflected the general lack of seriousness. It was all very slovenly, very dishonest and very degrading for someone who believed implicitly in Alfred de Vigny's '*Servitude et grandeur militaires*'.

In conclusion, even when I was a cadet, the republican régime appeared to me to be discredited from the military point of view. My political ideas changed when I was a second lieutenant. Strangely, however, I remained and continue to remain a republican.

CHAPTER III

Life at Military School under the régime

I HAVE already described my feelings of disillusion on first coming into contact with the Army under the republican régime, when I became cadet-sergeant in an artillery regiment and then a student at the Military School. I have also mentioned some of the clear symptoms of deterioration in discipline and in equipment which were discernible, in spite of the worthy intentions of the men who created the Republic.

At the Military School I grew to manhood in an atmosphere compounded partly of discipline, partly of youthful energy and fun—there are two sides to my temperament which some people appear to regard as revealing schizophrenic tendencies. And in fact although I observed service regulations scrupulously as a cadet, I was otherwise very full of mischief.

When one tries to draw up a scale of military values, equal gravity cannot be attached to the action of a cadet who climbs over the walls of his school at night to go and have a good time and enjoy life as to late arrival on parade, slackness in training, evasion of responsibility, or failure to conquer fear.

I loved life and I loved my friends and so from time to time I absented myself from the Military School whose stupid rules did not even give one the right to sleep out on Saturdays. To achieve this, I had to devise a very subtle technique. I used to leave a skilfully arranged dummy in my bed to deceive the duty officer when he went the rounds of the dormitories. On one occasion, unfortunately, the officer needed to speak with me after lights out, to give me an urgent message about drill for the following day. When he tried to wake me up, part of the dummy came away in his hand, and he realized that he had been tricked.

On one of these occasions, I strengthened the liking which Miguel Pereira Coutinho, Second Commandant of the School, had for me. He was at that time a lieutenant-colonel and is now a retired general. He insisted that I should explain my conduct, despite my unwillingness to do so. I told him that, unaware that I had been refused an all-night pass, I had entered into a solemn undertaking to spend the night outside the school, except in the event of an act of God. In view of the official refusal of leave, I thought that it would be a breach of my solemn undertaking were I to consider the fifteen-foot wall as an act of God. . . . The commandant found it hard to restrain a smile at my confession and did not punish me that time.

Ever since then despite my military correctness which some have considered—and still consider—exaggerated, my sensibilities as a practical, analytically minded man have been offended by that irksome, unnecessary and harmful restriction of not permitting cadets to sleep out on Saturday nights.

Similarly offensive to me was the evident preoccupation with subjecting the cadet to a ten-hour working day and to a stupid time-table which forced one to rush to and fro between theoretical lectures, lunch, gymnastics, fencing, horsemanship, rifle practice and sports, with hardly an hour free for one's own private concerns. The result was that one went around half-asleep with accumulated fatigue to such an extent that in some lectures, given by the more indulgent teachers, some students gave way to their drowsiness with loud, prolonged snores.

It was during this period that the idea took root in my mind that discipline and military protocol were perfectly compatible with good manners. To some extent though, good manners were incompatible with life in barracks which indeed puts a special stamp on any officer whose life is completely bound up with the barracks. A civilian cannot fail to notice some of the traits which mark officers of this type who, even in their vocabulary, so often limited and commonplace, slangy and cluttered with jargon, show only the crude, debased and medieval side of soldiering.

27

When I was a student, unfortunately a considerable number of the officers responsible for our training were of this type, always with the word 'no' on the tip of their tongue and with a devilish streak of sadism in their hearts. I was promoted very rapidly and when I became an officer in the Air Force and on the General Staff, I met some of them years later in the service when our relative positions were reversed and I was superior to them in rank. It made one sick to see the lion change into a snake, and not even a poisonous one at that.

I must not neglect to mention one side of my temperament and my proclivities which may have had some small part in influencing the Opposition to invite me to stand as a candidate for the office of President of the Republic at a difficult moment in our nation's history. I refer to my love of literature. I have produced little, not only from lack of the necessary abilities but also from lack of time, busy as I have been all my life and obliged to do several things at a time without remuneration or for merely nominal payment. As a reader, on the other hand, I read voraciously from the age of seven onwards when I started to devour those popular works of fiction that used to appear in instalments. Some of their titles linger vaguely in my memory. If I am not mistaken there were *Maria, Fairy of the Woods*, *The 145th Regiment*, *The Soldier and the Monk*, and others along similar lines, in a period when all noses were aquiline, teeth shone like pearls, vases were made of alabaster, faces were ruddy and the skies were always blue. There were also men who were fleet of foot, dishonoured noblemen, damsels in distress, duels, etc. . . . .

While at the Army School and in my early years as a junior officer, I continued to read avidly the books typical of that period, like Erich Maria Remarque's *All Quiet on the Western Front*, set against the background of the military tragedy of the First World War, or Victor Marguerite's *Garçonne*, with its picture of the revolution in manners and behaviour which followed that holocaust. This was a time when my comrades in the Artillery, and subsequently in the Air Force, used to tease me for being 'a man with a book always under his arm'.

From what has been said the reader will not be surprised

that from a very early age I should have begun to take an
interest in all aspects of national affairs, through the daily
press and through books. And this I did. I analysed and studied
the Republic—or rather, the succession of republican governments—when I was barely turned twenty.

The weakness of the régime

With the administrative inefficiency and the almost permanent disorders in the streets came attempts to assassinate
prominent personalities. It is possible that some republicans
speak with a modicum of truth when they try to find excuses
for this period and attribute the cause or the blame for these
outrages rather vaguely to 'enemies of the Republic'. The
argument is not convincing. If there had been a firm hand in
the Government and some honesty in parliament, these things
would not have happened. Besides, important personages of
the Republic deny the soundness of the excuse which, in any
event, is unacceptable legally. It would be better if we republicans—including those like me who had nothing to do with the
bankruptcy of the First Republic—were to accept facts without
thereby renouncing the desire to see a Republic, not a
Monarchy, as the proper system of government for Portugal.
It is not that one cannot have an excellent monarchical form
of democracy, as is the case in Britain and in the Scandinavian
countries, or a very bad republican form of government, as in
many parts of South America—to say nothing of Salazar's
republic. No: it is merely that one should be practical.

The régime was weakened at the outbreak of the First World
War due to the conflict of opinion between the parties as to
whether or not to take part in the war. Instability grew.
Between 1919 and 1926, there were three Presidents of the
Republic in the palace at Belém and twenty-six governments
in office! Quite a lot. No republican, whatever his age, can
possibly defend the tragic process of change which took place
in government.

Moreover, I have always experienced a sense of disgust at
the hyper-sensitivity still preserved even after all this time by
those persons who were dislodged in 1926. And very much so,
for I, a second lieutenant on the occasion of the '28th May

1926', constantly and without constraint attacked the path that revolt took.

Between 1920 and 1925 attempts were made to bring about a truce in matters of religion. Intolerance had been much in evidence in the case of the miracle at Fátima in 1917 which became a matter of political contention. In the interests of securing religious peace, the President of the Republic, Antonio José de Almeida, in 1920 placed the biretta of Cardinal on the head of Monsignor Locatelli, the Papal Nuncio in Lisbon, and Cardinal Antonio Belo was elected a permanent member of the Academy in 1923. Without exactly managing to win over those Catholics who were most adamantly opposed to it, the Republic did succeed in regaining the prestige which it originally had possessed.

A good idea of the state of the Republic in 1925 may be formed from a number of news items and comments fully justifying the coining of the verb *'portugaliser'*, current at the time. In the newspaper *A Noite* for 2nd June 1926, Cunha Leal, an important leader of the Opposition, wrote: 'Scandalous things are being done in public administration which provide every ground for constant smear campaigns.

'State-owned shipping, the *bairros sociais*,[1] the Rio de Janeiro exhibition—to mention merely some of the abuses which have most forcibly impressed public opinion—have become heaps of mud with which to foul the prestige of the State.'

Raul Proença wrote in *Seara Nova* for 15th July 1925: 'Local government councils are now like ante-rooms of banks and politics are a means of making one's fortune.' Finally, in the same publication on 27th October 1925, that patriarchal figure, Jaime Cortesão, remarked à propos of those republican councillors who defended the great commercial and industrial magnates and had gained themselves the name of 'lightning-conductors': 'There are a lot of them. And these "lightning-conductors" understand each other marvellously well. They protect one another and look after their mutual interests. One will go up to another and say—"I'm not going to say anything because that way I stand to gain a lot of money." The other replies—"Now you're talking, old man."

[1] *bairros sociais—disreputable areas.*

'And nothing is said. The vast majority of these men are going to be re-elected. The sovereign people are going to give them their votes and the shirts off their backs.'

In February 1927, less than a year after the fall of the Government, Jaime Cortesão turned against the military dictatorship—which shows to some extent how confused, from the practical point of view, was the position of the Portuguese politicians when the First Republic collapsed.

Unbalanced budgets, lack of proper accounts and confusion generally went on eating up all available resources. This happened, for example, to the money earned from the sale of silver when silver coins were withdrawn from circulation, and even to considerable loans obtained in London. It was like a leaking ship in terms of expenditure, and nothing was being collected by way of income.

Everything, both inside and outside the country, converged until all eyes were on the Army. On 18th April 1925 (I was as yet not an officer), the Armed Forces revolted in the first attempt to take civil power into their own hands and not merely to protect some political faction or other. Nevertheless, the composition of the insurgent group reminded one somewhat of the 'Sidonista'[1] movement. The revolt was immediately put down.

On 10th July in the same year, Captain Mendes Cabeçadas, one of the founders of the Republic when he was a young lieutenant, led an abortive revolt aboard the *Vasco da Gama*. The whole business was indicative of the state of affairs— one of the founding fathers unsheathing his sword against the 'rightfully chosen' government and against the parliament 'elected by the sovereign people'. Captain Cabeçadas, now a retired admiral, must also have been surfeited with governmental instability and incompetence.

He, too, probably looked back over the immediate past at the tremendous number of people who had been Ministers. For example, turning to statistics, the government of Alvaro de Castro lasted for 10 days in November 1920; that of Manuel P. Coelho, which followed, for 17 days; that of António

[1] The movement which seized power during the First World War, led by Sidónio Pais. (Translator)

Maria da Silva, for 23 days on one occasion and 20 on another; that of Genestal Machado, for 33 days; that of Maia Pinto, for 40 days; that of Victor Hugo de Azevedo Coutinho—a government popularly known as 'Les Misérables de Victor Hugo' —for 44 days; that of João Chagas, for 35 days; that of Antonio Granjo, for 50 days; and the government of Cunha Leal, for 52 days.

The government of Fernandes Costa, on 16th January 1920, ended before it even began, as a number of individuals, self-styled defenders of the purity of the Republic, prevented it from taking office. Up to 1925, including the government of António Maria da Silva, 193 citizens had held office as Ministers, making an average of 13 débuts per year or 1·09 a month. In 1920 alone there were eight governments and in 1921 no less than six.

One might wonder after all this whether it does not seem paradoxical on my part to remain a republican. Not at all. I recognize that despite everything the men who created the Republic allowed a clean wind to blow through Portuguese society, and the great men among them kept their hands clean while in office. Apart from that, the monarchical idea in Portugal besides representing for the mass of the people a retrogression constituted merely a tiresome irritation which tried occasionally to be something more than just that but had no real substance.

My life as a soldier

To change the subject for a while (and a change may well be acceptable) permit me to digress a little. I should like to dispel an idea which seems to exist, mainly abroad, that I represent a certain type of spare-time soldier with no great interest in soldiering due to political preoccupations. The very opposite is true. In fact I have had the reputation ever since I was a little boy of being 'crazy' about soldiering.

Those who are acquainted with me know my liking for drills, tactics and parades. They know, too, those outward signs—the vigorous salutes, the jangling spurs (which I wore in the Artillery) and my constant resistance in the Air Force to its tendency to water down military discipline.

As a colonel commanding a unit for a year, the transformation that I brought about in my regiment is common knowledge. I was greatly touched on one occasion to see the corporal of the guard sprinkling water on the ground where the sentry had to march up and down so that whenever I came in or went out of the post, there would not be any dust on the boots of the soldier on sentry duty. . . .

Promoted in 1925 to the rank of second lieutenant in the Artillery, I went to the Artillery training school, one of the few military establishments where discipline was maintained. Unfortunately, a sergeant whose political activities were notorious was transferred there from Lisbon by the Ministry of War. The consequence was that on the night of 2nd February 1926 there broke out in the school, utterly unexpectedly, a revolt of sergeants acting in concert with civilians. One by one they arrested the officers at dead of night.

As I was being marched off, disarmed and under guard, we met a detachment led by a sergeant. A soldier to the very marrow of my bones, although I was in a position where it was practically impossible to do anything, I glimpsed in a flash a way to end the revolt. I straightway evaded my guards and ran up to the sergeant leading the detachment to arrest him and relieve him of his command.

When I had gone three or four yards a shot hit me. It was at point-blank range and I fell in my tracks. When I came in the prison to take my clothes off so that the two bullet holes could be treated, the tiny revolver bullet was found. Strange how a mere 10 grammes of metal could bring me to the ground—by virtue of the fact that the momentum of the bullet, at such short range, was considerable, proportional as it is to the mass multiplied by the square of the velocity which, so close, would be about 300 metres per second. And in this way I was at the age of nineteen made a sort of national 'hero' by the newspapers.

The strange thing is that four months later I myself revolted against the Government which almost immediately suppressed the revolt, pursuing the rebels to Almada on the southern bank of the Tagus, opposite Lisbon. I became involved in a revolution in order to impose some order and not to create more disorder.

Why do I relate all this? Because this and other incidents in my eventful life are important stepping stones in the development of my outlook and consciousness as a soldier to the point where I could accept the revolution of 1926, against the civil authority, as being legitimate.

An army does not become disciplined overnight and so in the early days of the dictatorship I was to find vestiges of the low level of discipline and equipment, which had typified the last years of the Republic, in the Independent Bomber Group of the Air Force—the first unit in which I served as a pilot. It outraged my soldier's spirit.

One could get to Alverca from Lisbon by about 10 a.m., make a short flight if aircraft and petrol were available, and at midday set off again for Lisbon. . . .

The unit had at its disposal only three or four aircraft, old and rarely available for use. When I arrived none of them could be flown. With all a young pilot's enthusiasm I borrowed an aeroplane from the Air Force supply depot. They had only one and it lacked a speedometer.

In those days I did not consider that the lack of a speedometer—that indispensable instrument for measuring speed, the force which alone holds aircraft in the sky—stood in the way of flying. The consequence was that about 200 metres off the ground I stalled and crashed. The aeroplane burst into flames. I felt one foot burning and tugged violently at it, managing to get my left boot off and leaving it there to burn. I crashed near the entrance to the Air Force depot and the guard there ran up in time to cut my safety-belt and save my life.

The position was similar with regard to discipline. The man who really commanded the unit was a sergeant-major with whom the two commanding officers, his superiors in rank, shook hands every day! A position like this was quite unbearable to my sense of military etiquette. It may have been a whim of destiny to make me the officer provisionally commanding a squadron, thus bringing the sergeant in question under my direct authority. He was so important that he had permanently installed in his house a private soldier who was a baker in civilian life and who in his army life ran a baker's shop for the sergeant! I punished the sergeant shortly afterwards despite terrible pressure against such a course, due to the protection he enjoyed from the two commanding officers of the unit. It put a severe strain on my sense of honesty and dedication to the service.

The prelude to the final collapse

Let us take up the thread again, from the skein of intrigue and confusion. After the revolts in 1925 the final collapse of the Government was in practically everyone's mind. Dr José Domingos dos Santos, who had brought about the split in the Democratic party, prophesied in an interview with the *Diário de Lisboa* that General Bernard Faria, who was expected to lead a government, would be allowed by the Head of the State to dissolve parliament so that he could govern without being subjected to criticism and reproach. I had ample excuse for taking part, at the age of twenty, in the revolution of 28th May 1926.

When the rebels of 18th April 1925 were judged, the moving spirit behind that revolt was found to be General Carmona, who later became President of the Republic for a very long time, over twenty years, under military dictatorship. I had known him when he commanded the Cavalry Training School at Torres Novas and I was only ten. I was an observant child and it was when I went round with my father who was at that time supplies officer at Torres Novas, that I heard people criticize Carmona's weakness as a commanding officer. But as a leading figure in the revolt he acquired plenty of courage and said before the court what was on everyone's lips—'Our motherland is sick'. Because of this he was to become President of the Republic, but a President devoid of power, although according to some journalists he was a great statesman!

Absolutely indicative of the state of mind of the Armed Forces and of the whole country was the pardon granted to the rebels of the 18th April revolt, who had not denied their guilt.

After all the events that have been described, it was not difficult to foresee that the Army could come out of its barracks and seize power whenever it liked and without a shot being fired. And it did come out. On 28th May 1926.

CHAPTER IV

The revolt of 28th May 1926
and its aftermath

TOWARDS the end of 1925 or early in 1926, I came into touch for the first time with those officers who had been transferred to the 1st Artillery Regiment at Évora from the Lisbon garrison because they had taken part in the revolt on 18th April 1925. I was then nineteen years old, a second lieutenant under training at the Artillery School at Vendas Novas, at the end of my course at the Army School. At weekends we all used to meet one another in the train to Lisbon and it was here that I came to know about the movement and the preparations it was making.

After the revolt of sergeants and civilians which I had opposed and in which, as I have recounted, I was wounded, training was speeded up and the young officers were scattered among the various Artillery regiments.

I was posted to the Horse Artillery batteries at Queluz (Lisbon), under the command of Lieutenant-Colonel Malheiro. This unit evidently enjoyed the complete confidence of the Government despite the fact that some of its officers had revolted on 18th April 1925.

The Air Force had about fifty officers when recruitment was resumed in 1926 after six years or so without any intake of new blood. The select company of fliers was at that time made up mainly of a very uninhibited type of individual little given to intellectual discussion and totally unconcerned with discipline. A considerable number of them came from the Cavalry as for example the then Captain Craveiro Lopes, who was to become President of the Republic and whom I knew intimately as an instructor.

I shall come back later and discuss this contact. For the moment I shall merely say that when the military government got under way I, although promoted to an Artillery officer months before, was in fact attending the Air Force Training School as a trainee pilot. The School operated then —and still does—at the foot of the beautiful range of mountains in the triangle of tourist country formed by Sintra-Cascais-Mafra.

In the last-named town, about ten kilometres distant from Sintra, was the Infantry Training School with a very large establishment. Accompanied by two lieutenants I went to try and persuade its commanding officer to join the movement which had started at Braga in the north of Portugal under the leadership of General Gomes da Costa. I shall come back to this later on.

The disorganization and collapse of morale that was affecting the Army has already been described. Small wonder then that the subalterns—the heart and soul of the movement—found it extremely difficult to find a general prepared to lead them in the attempt to overthrow the Government. Eventually they found a leader in General Gomes da Costa. From that intensely Catholic city of Braga, General Gomes da Costa issued his first proclamation to the country. Couched in sober terms it ran as follows:

'Portuguese! For men of dignity and honour the political situation of the country is inadmissible. Bowed low by the actions of a licentious and tyrannical minority, the nation is shamed and feels as though it is dying. As for me, I openly revolt. And let all men of courage and dignity come with me, arms in hand, to conquer or die by my side. To arms, Portugal! To arms, Portugal, for Liberty and for the honour of the nation!

'To arms, Portugal!
Gomes da Costa
Commander-in-chief of the National Army.'

This is an appropriate moment in which to refer to a photocopied document that I possess which bears a number of signatures and initials of officers from the rank of colonel down to that of second lieutenant. It comprises seven articles and seven principles which represent the ideas of the officers involved in the 28th May movement. Article 1 reads as follows:

'The undersigned, officers of the garrison at ——, pledge themselves on their honour to collaborate in a movement exclusively national in character, having as its object the return of normality in political life and the restoration of the prestige of the Republic which they recognize and will defend as a legally constituted system of Government.'

Article 3 reads:

'The Government constituted shall remain in power for as long as may be necessary to effect the country's restoration to moral and administrative health, in accordance with the general principles outlined in the document appended to this agreement, forming an integral part of it and to be initialled by the officers signing this agreement.'

The document states in article 2 that the head of the Government should be a general or some other senior officer of the Army or the Navy, 'of undoubted republican loyalties and irreproachable character'.

Among the signatures which are still legible is that of Commander José Mendes Cabeçadas of the Navy who was the first Prime Minister, although a theorist and at loggerheads with the leader of the revolt, General Gomes da Costa, as we shall see later on.

A number of important basic points deserve special mention:

a) Strict rules of conduct for civil servants and the dismissal of redundant officials.

b) Transfer of the State-owned railways to private enterprise.

c) Changes in the control of the match and tobacco industries so that the State would reap the benefit to which it is entitled.

d) Survey and registration of landed property.

e) Reorganization of the Army and the Navy in such a way as to enhance the prestige of military institutions and to guarantee the efficient defence of Portugal herself and of her colonies.

f) Reform of the educational system with an increase in the number of primary schools.

g) Application of moral principles in the legal system.

h) Revision of the law of leasehold.

i) A law governing the press, combining liberty with safeguards for the moral integrity of individuals.

j) Reform of the Ministry of Colonies and the preparation of a code of rules governing the appointment of High Commissioners and other officials, preparation of a plan for colonial development, and the inception of measures to promote emigration to the colonies.

k) Creation of funds for the relief of workers who are disabled or in ill-health.

Gomes da Costa arrived at Braga with his adjutants in a borrowed Cadillac and proceeded to make contact with officers of the 8th, 11th and 29th Infantry. Among the dozen or so officers involved was Captain Gonçalves da Silva.

Some of the officers mentioned belonged to the Revolutionary Junta which was set up secretly on 10th January 1926, four months before the revolt. Attempts at counteraction on the part of the two divisional commanders, General Domingues Peres and General Souza Dias, were abortive. The whole body of officers was either involved in events or imbued with a spirit of indiscipline, seeing the Army constantly embroiled in petty revolutions with its barracks under attack by civilians and sometimes having officers leading it who were more concerned with making a career for themselves outside than inside the Armed Forces.

While Gomes da Costa acted more like a soldier than a politician, trying to steer a middle course which would be acceptable to all shades of Army opinion—as may be seen in the document which I have already quoted—Commander Mendes Cabeçadas in Lisbon acted more like a politician than a naval officer and presented the following communication to the President of the Republic:

'Officers representing the overwhelming majority of the Army have charged me with the duty of communicating to your Excellency their strong desire that the present political situation be resolved by Your Excellency's appointment of a government of non-party composition and made up of republicans deserving of the confidence of the country.

'In making this request the Army is sure that it is expressing the feelings of the nation.'

With regard to low pay and the Army's noble acceptance of a rather stiff 'public recovery' tax, I can recall the words of a man much in the public view at the time—Commander Ochoa of the Navy—who remarked: 'A few days ago someone tried to buy the Army for two or three hundred escudos, as though the Army was something that could be bought and sold.' In reaction against the increasing of salaries by the Democratic Government in power, I was one of those who advocated that the 'public recovery' tax should take a higher percentage from the Army than from civil servants.

General Carmona, later to be President of the Republic for twenty-three years, behaved in a rather strange manner. When he was invited to join the revolutionary movement, just as he was leaving for Alentejo on a routine trip as Inspector of Cavalry, he considered the arguments advanced by Commander Cabeçadas to be inadequate. The revolt broke out in the north while he was in Elvas. And then the true nature of the peace-time general came to light, making it easy to understand how he became a mere puppet in Salazar's hands. As usual, the general went to the Elvas railway station in order to return to Lisbon. He presented his travel warrants which the station master refused to accept, acting on general instructions from Lisbon. One officer presented his identity card instead of a travel warrant and got a ticket at the usual considerable reduction in price. He would get a refund later. But what does the worthy Carmona do? He lets the train go through and returns to his hotel.

O tempora! O mores!

He finally joined in later, on 30th May, when practically the whole of the Army was heart and soul with the movement or, at least, had no possibility of backing out.

The Democratic Government resigned and then there began another sort of muddle. Everybody sought to give orders to the Forces and advice to the President of the Republic. There were no less than two military committees in Lisbon —the 'white' and the 'green'—both pontificating away to the 'top brass' who seemed quite ready to accept ideas from both of them!

One very politically minded naval officer, Commander Procópio de Freitas, even occupied the Ministry of the Navy and gave arms to civilian workers at the arsenal in order to establish a government along his own lines!

What a wonderful play is yet unwritten!

On the 30th, Dr Bernadino Machado, President of the Republic, invited Commander Mendes Cabeçadas to form a government. Discussions were held on the 31st with the lieutenant sent to represent General Gomes da Costa, and agreement was reached on the composition of the first government. The post of Minister of War went to Gomes da Costa and that of Minister of the Interior to Mendes Cabeçadas, who then declared that he had not resigned from the Republican Liberal Union (*União Liberal Republicana*) to which he 'was proud to belong'.

This declaration was like a red rag to a bull for the young men in the Armed Forces who at the time, with or without reason, hated all politicians impartially.

The silent war between Gomes da Costa and Cabeçadas began. The latter ordered the release of a number of eminent political prisoners held at the Entroncamento (80 kilometres north-east of Lisbon), but Gomes da Costa countermanded the order.

At the same time the general decided to march on Lisbon and telegraphed the units stationed there to inform them that the Lisbon Government was unworthy of their confidence. The concentration of forces loyal to Gomes da Costa began.

On 31st May the President of the Republic resigned.

This is the point at which to say something about myself.

Before the President's resignation I, then an Artillery second lieutenant studying at the Air Force School, resolved to act on my own initiative in the absence of orders. Full of enthusiasm I put forward ideas and proposed things to do.

The result of these discussions was that, accompanied by two lieutenants, I went to Mafra where the Infantry Training School was located, to persuade that establishment to join us.

The commanding officer, Colonel Oliveira Gomes, turned quite pale when I told him that we could not stay for very long as any delay would be taken to mean that we had been arrested and then planes would come and bomb the Training School. (There weren't any bombs. . . .) Afterwards, when the officers were assembled, he almost fainted in my arms from the 'great responsibility' that he felt.

The poor man eventually made up his mind. I then became a go-between, the link between that establishment and the Air Force School. In Sintra I met Sarmento Beires who had taken over command, as the commanding officer had gone home. . . . From Sintra we went to Amadora, an insignificant little town some six kilometres or so from Lisbon, where a number of Air Force squadrons were based.

Oliveira Gomes, his composure regained, was one of the delegates that Cabeçadas sent to meet Gomes da Costa. It was agreed that government should be exercised by a triumvirate composed of Commander Cabeçadas, General Gomes da Costa and Commander Ochoa. Each of them took on several portfolios, with the General holding three—those of War, Colonies and Agriculture. This was really quite easy as nobody did anything. Two of the ministers weren't in Lisbon in any case. . . .

Gomes da Costa on the warpath

Events became even more like an operetta by Offenbach! Gomes da Costa sent out a telegram to the Armed Forces saying that he disagreed with the way in which the Govern-

43

ment was organized and that the distribution of portfolios that had been announced was incorrect. And in his best barrack-room manner he told the press: 'Just fancy! Me, the Minister of Agriculture. I'm going to deal with potatoes now!'

Gomes da Costa left Coimbra for Sacavem (fifteen kilometres north-east of Lisbon) and there at last a government was formed with at least some semblance of stability. It had nine ministers, among then Dr Salazar—although in name alone, as I shall be explaining later. Cabeçadas was Prime Minister and Gomes da Costa Minister of War.

Spectacle and pageantry are indispensable in such matters and so on Sunday, 6th June, a great military parade took place in Lisbon with Gomes da Costa, a fine figure of a man, on horseback at its head. I was the standard-bearer of the Air Force contingent.

When he took over the portfolio of Minister of War, Gomes da Costa ordered the release of the prisoners taken as a consequence of the revolt of 2nd February at Vendas Novas —the action already mentioned, in the course of which I was shot and wounded by one of the sergeants implicated in the revolt.

I shall not argue the case here, but to my military mind it was a most undesirable thing for sergeants to be allowed to think that they could so unceremoniously fire at officers —and at unarmed officers at that, as in my case. I twice raised the matter formally through official channels but got no satisfaction. Accordingly I got into the train and travelled to Vizeu (to the 7th Artillery) where the sergeant who had shot me was stationed.

I invited him into the library and in two minutes settled my score with him. He was taken off to hospital with an assortment of bruises from the hiding I gave him. Not wishing to sacrifice my career as a flier for my misdeeds, I got on the train back to Lisbon, before they could arrest me.

When I had to answer to a court-martial for the crime I had committed, I asked Lieutenant-Colonel Costa Ferreira, formerly my Professor of Ballistics, to defend me. Tall, heavily built, and weighed down with medals, this most distinguished officer inspired respect. (Shortly afterwards he was to become Minister of Education taking me with him as his secretary. A very liberal-minded republican, he was a Minister for only a short while in the government which included Dr Salazar as Minister of Finance. I was Ferreira's secretary for barely two months, from 12th September to 14th November, 1929.)

In the courtroom at my trial, Costa Ferreira said that his dearest wish was that his son should be 'like the noble officer now sitting in the dock as the defendant'. I was acquitted!

On 12th June 1926 Gomes da Costa announced that he was again taking up arms, this time to drive out Cabeçadas who tried to resist but had no backing and was ousted on 17th June. This was the first *coup d'état*.

The second *coup d'état* took place on 9th July. Gomes da Costa lacked the culture and balance necessary for high office, having been chosen mainly with regard to his military capabilities. He was exiled to the Azores on 11th July and ten days later was promoted to the rank of marshal. General Carmona, whom Gomes da Costa had nicknamed 'Rosy' (*róseo*), became Prime Minister.

Meanwhile the former politicians and the officers associated with them were busy plotting and intriguing. On 3rd February 1927 the bloody revolt in Oporto led by General Souza Dias broke out, less than a year since the overthrow of the Democratic Government by the Army. Energetically leading the attack, on behalf of the newly established dictatorial government, was its Minister of War, Lieutenant-Colonel Passos e Souza.

Firing ceased only at dawn on 8th February.

In the meantime a revolt had also broken out in Lisbon on the 7th, led by a courageous, politically minded naval officer, Commander Agatão Lança. The Largo do Rato, now called the Praça do Brasil, was the scene of much of the shooting. Still under training as a pilot, I volunteered for active service and marched up with thirty airmen and two other officers, one of whom I never saw again until the revolt was over. We manned barricades in the Rua São Felipe Neri, one of the streets leading to that ill-fated square.

45

How wild and cruel man can become!

A field-gun had been left behind in the Largo do Rato. From the nearby corner the enemy were trying to drag it over to their side by means of a rope. With another officer I ran from door to door as far as the corner and from there, throwing hand grenades at right angles to our left, we wiped out those who had been getting on our nerves with their 'rope tricks'. The whole business was really very cruel.

Man is the most paradoxical of all animals. Helped by two of my men, I went to the rescue of a cat abandoned when its owners fled to safety and which was without food or water. This also took place under fire, which further impressed the irrational. . . .

Nearby, Lieutenant Henrique Galvão was fighting gallantly.

The rebels surrendered after fifty-three hours of fighting.

On 30th September 1927 the National Union (*União Nacional*) was formed, the beginning of one-party rule. On 30th November Salazar began to publish a series of carefully considered articles on Portugal's financial problems, in the Catholic newspaper *As Novidades*. The *Diário de Notícias* for 14th December refers to them in terms of the highest praise and points out that the deficit, on a budget of 1,300,000 contos, was 689,000 contos, or over 50%, in the first year of the dictatorship, June 1926 to June 1927.

In the natural anxiety to give some semblance of legality to the dictatorship, Carmona was elected President of the Republic, unopposed, with 738,065 votes, his inauguration taking place on 15th April 1928.

Dr Salazar, who legally held the portfolio of Minister of Finance from 30th May to 30th July 1926, in fact spent only a few days in office, being unable to stand the topsy-turvy atmosphere of which some idea has been given in the foregoing pages. He comes back into the picture again when he assumed real power on 28th April 1928.

The great hope was born. How well I remember it! Hope that was to be transformed into a great calamity—as I see it.

CHAPTER V

Impressions of university life
and experiences in Africa

THE course in military engineering took seven years, after secondary school, and comprised three years of university studies and four years at the Army School. I actually enrolled for it at the University of Coimbra. Then, anxious to begin my military life sooner, I decided to start at the Army School and take a simpler course there. The result was that hardly had I put up my insignia as an Artillery Second Lieutenant, when I felt dissatisfied on two counts—in my pride and with the state of my knowledge.

Although the Army School provided the rudiments of a number of 'civilian' university subjects such as descriptive geometry, calculus of probabilities and others indispensable for the understanding of some military sciences, in fact I felt a certain deficiency in my basic education when I spread my wings, and set about learning as much as I could about the things that interested me. Mathematics were my weakest point.

As for my pride, during the course itself I was conscious of the half-scornful way in which my colleagues in the secondary course, although invariably worse qualified than I, used to look at me merely because they were enrolled in the 'civilian' University where I was never actually to become a student myself.

My passionate desire for knowledge, which was to lead me to the University when I had become an Air Force officer,

47

increased when I left the Artillery and started training as a
flier from 1926 to 1928.

I got very upset by the incompetence of some of the science
instructors. Some of them had not even finished secondary
school, which meant that it was a waste of time for me to ask
questions, since their unscientific minds were not equipped
for analysis but only for accepting without discussion what
the books told them.

The Air Force recruited very few officers with scientific
attainments. On the contrary, it tended to get a high proportion of its personnel from the Cavalry. It also included in its
ranks many officers who were not regulars but had managed
to stay in the Army by taking the course of training for pilots
—at that time a course about on the sergeant level in which
riding instructors were able to join as well if they wished.
It will readily be appreciated that this was not the most
attractive of atmospheres for anyone with my kind of specu-
lative, intellectual mind.

Feeling out of my element, in 1929 I enrolled at the University of Lisbon. I studied in the faculties of Science, Letters
and Law, but spent most of my time in the first. During
this time, although I was a student whose connection with
the Armed Forces was limited to my flying activities, I was
very sad to see some officers who were enrolled in the University quite shamelessly cutting sorry figures in their classes,
though it pained me a great deal to see the civilian students,
many of them considerably younger, making fun of the
Army officers sitting with them in the lecture halls. More
than once there were delicate situations in the University
when guarded gibes were made against the political set-up
in the Army. 'One of them,' they used to say in the corridors,
meaning the Army. In uniform, some six years or so older
than the average student, I represented a kind of blemish
on the academic scene.

I have advocated, and continue to advocate, these preliminary years of university work, although they are not as
onerous now as they were in my day, and I do so particularly
for countries which are not constantly faced by the threat
of war and where, as a result, the Army tends to get turned

into a kind of modern equivalent of the monasteries of the seventeenth century, namely, a home for penurious and stupid young men of good family.

But the point that I want to make is that the fact that I did very well in my university work, as a young lieutenant, brought me a good deal of esteem twenty years later, when I was a candidate for the Presidency, among intellectuals in various professions who had been fellow students of mine in one or other of the three faculties mentioned. They remembered their fellow-student from the Army who had not made a bad showing in the University. At the very least they did not attribute to me either of the two characteristics that civilians tend to ascribe to soldiers: indolence and stupidity. I was one of their own kind. Anyway, I applied myself to my studies in the most exemplary fashion.

As for the competence and quality of the academic staff, I want to make a few comments in these reminiscences of mine. In the Faculty of Science I met no professors who did not come up to the high standards which should be characteristic of university education. I must modify that statement —I did meet one, who was incompetent. He was an exception.

Regrettably, the same did not apply in the Faculties of Letters and Law. The lack of seriousness in examinations was appalling, and some of the professors turned a blind eye to it. Some of the courses were also of pitifully poor quality. Despite the meagreness and simplicity of the lectures, curiously enough a goodly number of my civilian fellow-students were filled with terror of being asked questions in class. I still laugh heartily when I think of a little comedy that used to take place every winter. There was no form of heating provided and so we were obliged to wear our coats and scarves in order to keep warm. When I wore my military cape—which was sleeveless and when spread out hid a great area from the professor's sight—the student sitting behind me used to say 'Lieutenant, spread out your cape'. In this way, that future lawyer used to try to evade the professor's eye and so avoid being asked questions.

Worse than that, however, was what used to happen on

the eve of examinations. One of my young civilian fellow-students asked me whether I had been to the professor's house yet.

'Why?'

'Oh. Don't you know?'

'No.'

'To ask him to be lenient.'

That was in 1933 at the height of the dictatorship.

In the Faculty of Letters I was to find, side by side with some serious and responsible type (as there were in the Law faculty as well), a thoroughly disillusioning number of professors who gave their teaching neither the depth nor the seriousness and high quality that I believe should be expected. Some professors set no examinations at all while others used to leave the examination room in the middle of a written test, with the results that one might expect from students of Latin extraction. Even I was invited to give a lecture, and the professor did me the honour of getting me to repeat it before the Geographical Society of Lisbon nearly thirty years ago.

From my acquaintance with the three faculties the conviction took root in my mind that it must be very detrimental to political life for it to have fewer scientists than graduates in Law or Letters. Indeed, I came to the conclusion that the Faculties of Letters and Law, more than the Faculty of Science, were tainted with some noxious virus which weakened the character, due to the low standard of academic honesty and integrity which prevailed in them.

Feeling that some of the dreams that I had as an earnest little boy, when I so passionately chose a military career, were being dissipated in a country which had not experienced war for some years, I was nearly at the point of changing my mind about my career. Suddenly I thought of doing a medical course, and this when I was getting on for twenty-five years old and was an Air Force lieutenant. I was already attending courses in the basic subjects (physics, chemistry, botany and zoology) in conjunction with the General Staff course. Pride or vanity, however, influenced my final decision and I did not enrol in the medical school. If I could have become a doctor at a 'record' age, like twenty-two, that would have been one thing, but this would mean I should not graduate until the age of thirty, far behind my contemporaries.

By the time I was twenty-one I was already writing for the Portuguese press and in military technical journals. The fact of having been shot and wounded helped to draw the attention of our little country to the young officer who appeared to be an aspiring intellectual and a man of all-round ability. Having been a member of the 28th May movement and the youngest officer in the General Staff corps, the Government very naturally grabbed hold of me for the various 'para-military' organizations of a political nature which are one of the characteristic features of totalitarian régimes, both of the right and of the left, and through which they seek to regiment, by the fascination of wearing a uniform, young people and older persons who have either not done or have already completed their military service. Obviously they did not put me in charge but merely used me as a military adviser.

Even this did not altogether suit them, my period in office being rather brief.

In 1938—I was at that time the only Air Force officer who had taken the General Staff course—I was appointed a member of the Military Mission to the Colonies, which was charged with the duty of visiting the colonial territories and with making proposals for improving their defence arrangements.

The mission went out in the dry season and came back when the rainy season was about to begin. In Angola I covered thousands of kilometres, travelling from the Congo River to the provinces of Benguela and Huíla and right into the depths of the interior, to Malange and the inhospitable Bié province. I went by air to explore the Cunene River, including that part of it which, on the map of Angola that I had, was shown by dotted lines being, it was said, an area which the topographers had not yet visited on foot. In Mozambique, by car and on foot, I visited the districts of Lourenço Marques, Gaza, Inhambane, Manica and Sofala,

Tete, Zambésia, Mozambique and Cabo Delgado. I went through the district of Niassa by car and by air (exploring the uninhabited Rovuma River region) then proceeded via Zomba and Blantyre in Nyasaland, to the Rhodesias and the Union of South Africa. This mission alone would provide material for a book of memoirs as long as this one. Later on one of my chapters will deal further with the colonial question. For the moment I confine myself, in the space of a couple of dozen lines, to 'integrating' in as mathematical a sense as possible all the hundreds of impressions gained in the course of such a long journey which, although undertaken with military purposes in mind, nevertheless afforded many opportunities for contacts with the natives and with the civil authorities.

Here is a series of clear, enlightening 'snapshot' pictures:

The first is on board ship at São Tomé. As President Carmona was shortly due to visit the colonies, they were repatriating some of the black Africans who many years before had 'volunteered' to leave Angola for work in São Tomé. Wanting to know about everything, as usual, I went over to talk with them. They were on board the same ship as I was. Human scarecrows in rags, they were going to their deaths, for they had lost touch with their villages, the only real 'homeland' for the native in the tribal state.

The second is from the officers' mess at Luanda. One of the waiters, a Negro from the Cape Verde Islands, when he saw my practice of talking with the natives, very humbly begged me to concern myself with his case which nobody wanted to bother about. A convict, he had long ago served his sentence but nevertheless had not been sent back home because his name had been left off the list by mistake.

The third was confided to me by my batman, a Negro and the best soldier, black or white, ever to serve me in that capacity. He told me that he knew of an African chief who ate his baby daughter when she died from some disease.

The fourth is something I learned later from the confession of a colleague on that military mission to the colonies, to the effect that in a certain part of Angola when he asked for a black woman they produced for him a child who was already nubile. She wore a religious medallion around her neck, for the poor little thing had belonged to a Catholic mission whence, obviously in defiance of the rules and the wishes of the missionaries, the little girls were removed for that purpose. The most curious part of it all was that the local authorities did the same. . . . I asked: 'Suppose they become pregnant?' The reply was quite brutal: 'That's the girls' business.' Poor black girls!

The fifth is coloured by the respect which is inspired by the bush country, the *Sertão*, deep in the interior. Respect, not to say fear. I made a note of the date, so greatly was I appalled by the stupidity which I witnessed. It was after dark on 29th September 1939. We were between Porto Amélia and Quissanga in Mozambique.

The military convoy—two light cars, a small truck and a heavy lorry—by chance came upon a damaged vehicle with two Dutch priests and two nuns in it. They signalled us to stop and asked us to be kind enough to take them to a nearby German plantation where they would sleep and then attend to the damage in the morning. Our *chef de mission* looked at his watch. For a man who devoted three-quarters of his life to thinking about his belly it was already long past dinner-time. And so he left the priests and the nuns on the roadside, abandoning them to their fate!

The sixth concerns racial prejudice, rather paradoxical in anyone who used little black girls as wives. We were all extremely thirsty and ravenously hungry. The convoy stopped for a picnic meal because it was getting late. There were only enough glasses for the white men. One of the two black men with us sat watching the captain 'O.C. baggage', his eyes longingly following each drop that the latter poured down his throat. I said to the captain: 'Give that poor fellow a drop . . .' He answered angrily: 'No black man is going to drink out of my glass!' I clinched the matter by saying: 'Then he can drink out of mine. Soap washes everything clean.'

The seventh was one of the most shameful episodes in terms of tyrannical behaviour and lack of character that I ever saw in the whole of my military career. It occurred in Lumbo,

E   53

the curious island in the district of the same name, not far from the town of Mozambique. Our *chef de mission* was inspecting the armaments depot under the command of Lieutenant Carrington da Fonseca. With his usual stupidity, our brigadier started talking nonsense and told the lieutenant to inform the military commander of the colony that he, the brigadier, deplored the fact that the depot had a staff of only seven soldiers and had no motor transport or telephone.

The lieutenant did as he was ordered and despatched the message. Colonel Pinto da Silva, the military commander in Lourenço Marques, foamed with rage at this criticism, conveyed moreover through a subordinate. He remonstrated angrily with the brigadier. The latter, thinking things over and fearing that his general's stars might be in danger were there to be any repercussions in Lisbon, quite simply decided to sacrifice the poor lieutenant and to lie about the whole affair. *He denied that he had given the order to his subordinate at all.* Colonel Pinto da Silva punished the lieutenant with one day in prison for having been untruthful. The lieutenant lodged an appeal. (I, having been one of the several witnesses of the scene at Lumbo, wrote to him offering to testify against the abominable brigadier.) Whereupon the punishment was amended to 'censure' upon the lieutenant for 'not having made representations to the brigadier, pointing out that the order that he was giving was inappropriate'!

The reader may be wondering whether I saw nothing but immorality and degradation in those vast territories discovered and colonized by the Portuguese? I certainly did not.

Had our country not still been living in medieval times when the winds of a new age were blowing in Africa, Portugal would now be having fewer problems in her overseas territories.

PART TWO

CHAPTER VI

Dr Salazar, and my mission in the Azores

A GREAT deal has been written by fanatics both for and against this man, but one knows only too well how much accuracy to expect from political invective For my part it would be foolish to consider myself as a highly privileged exception to the general rule. Nevertheless I should like to point out that I have never received any personal affront from Dr Salazar. On the contrary, he himself suggested, without any solicitation on my part, offering me some of the various offices, including the two civilian ones, which I have held in connection with my profession. Through him I became Director-General of Civil Aviation for the first time in 1944 and later, only a short while after I had asked to be relieved of this office, he made me Portuguese representative at the International Civil Aviation Organization (I.C.A.O.) in Canada in 1947.

Yet I must state that the posts I held in Portugal either carried no salary at all or a ridiculously small one, averaging over a year something less than 750 escudos a month—the same as an ex-army lieutenant would get in the police force. As for the posts abroad which the dictator insinuated were mere sinecures, I must put on record that in every country I went to the sum I received for my work plus expenses was always less than the basic salary of one of its own nationals of equal rank. In Washington, for example, I was in the wretched position of receiving a salary amounting to some $400 a month less than an American general. Incidentally, the number of generals in the American Air Force, some three hundred, exceeded the Portuguese total of pilots.

Yet there were plenty of envious persons who would have loved to be nominated for the post, in spite of all its disadvantages, just for the pleasure of travelling and boosting their vanity.

Regarding Salazar's attitude towards me, I shall go even further and say that he has allowed me to express strong disagreement with him which perhaps is due to the sincerity and dedication with which I always served him. As an example I shall quote an extract from a memorandum of 13th November 1946 when I knew he was furious with me. I wrote: 'No one could deny that I have always served Your Excellency with the utmost respect and even personal devotion in spite of your habitual coldness towards your subordinates, but I must confess that I cannot offer my services in an atmosphere of fear and subservience.' I shall explain this in detail later.

I should add that in contrast to the general opinion of politicians I myself continue to believe that Salazar rendered the country a great service initially by bringing order into financial chaos.

He comes from a family of small farmers and was born on 28th April, 1889 (I wonder what astrologists could tell the Opposition about this date?) in a small village in the province of Beira Alta. He spent a restricted youth in the seminary of Vizeu where he studied for eight years before deciding to give up an ecclesiastical career. In 1914 he graduated in law with distinction and four years later became Professor of Political Economy in the University of Coimbra, doing a little writing for a limited public. When, in 1919, he was accused of monarchist tendencies and risked losing his chair, he showed his spirit by writing *My Reply* in which he declared his gratitude to the seminary which had maintained him 'almost free of cost'. In 1921 he became a deputy of the Catholic Centre party, but his public appearances can be counted on one's fingers—this was too noisy a business for a scholar!

He grew interested in the Portuguese economy and in

1923 wrote *The Reduction of Public Expenditure*. As I have already mentioned, in 1926 at the beginning of the dictatorship he was invited to be Finance Minister, but he only remained in office a few days for the political imbroglio was more than a man of his character could stand.

General Sinel de Cordes, the Finance Minister during the military dictatorship, was unable to remedy the state of this department, the nerve-centre of the Republic, for the year 1922/3 showed a deficit of 293,000 contos on a budget of 279,000. In the first year of the dictatorship, 1926/7, this deficit shot up to 642,000 contos and in the next year increased by a further 181,000. The floating debt rose by 475,000 contos in 1926/7 and another 178,000 in 1927/8. It was a gloomy picture for a backward country with its currency devalued and no growth in taxable products. Some suggested seeking a loan from the League of Nations but its conditions were extremely severe, partly because the country inspired little confidence financially and also because the opposition, the Paris League, did all they could to sabotage the idea. In fact it was even suggested that a commission of three foreigners should be set up to control public income. After this the matter went no further for, as the provisional Finance Minister, General Ivens Ferraz, said: 'Portugal is not going to sell herself for the sake of twelve million pounds.' The people were wildly enthusiastic and I remember pictures in the newspapers showing patriots offering articles of gold to help save their country. The increased circulation of paper money served to devalue the escudo still more. There were echoes of 'Sebastianism', the belief dating from 1578, when the poor, crazy King Sebastian died, burying his country's independence in the sands of Alcacer Quibir, but leaving behind among the Portuguese people the belief that he would return 'one misty morning'. D. Sebastian was to be resurrected in the person of Salazar.

On 15th April 1928 General Carmona, who had been elected unopposed on 25th March, was proclaimed President of the Republic and formed his government with General Vicente de Freitas as Prime Minister. Salazar was invited back and took up office on 27th April but, taking advantage of the circumstances, he agreed to accept only under strict conditions which in fact were to pave the way to his dictatorship. He insisted on the right to veto any increase in current expenditure, as well as any outlay on development for which credit facilities might not be available, and also to fix the budget of each ministry.

At that time I was a lieutenant pilot and I remember very well the wave of enthusiasm which his inauguration speech caused throughout the country; even the jokes about him showed a certain respect.

How different those speeches look today as I re-read them thirty years later. This was how he talked on 28th May, the second anniversary of the National Revolution: 'They say I have very delicate health, and yet I am never ill; they say my capacity for work is limited, and yet I work unceasingly. What is the explanation of this miracle? Simply the many good souls in Portugal who ardently hope and pray that I may continue in my task.' He finished on a poetic, patriotic note: 'This is the painful ascent to Calvary; at its summit men may die, but they redeem their motherland.'

In July 1929 there was another ministerial crisis, caused by an issue connected with religious processions, and Salazar resigned from one office only to accept another in the new government. There were rumours of changes, revolts and ministries followed one after the other, but still Salazar stayed on. In the ministry of November 1928 Quintão Meireles (now an Admiral) was briefly Minister of Foreign Affairs, which was the main reason why he was unexpectedly invited by the Opposition in 1951 to be their candidate for the Presidency. In another, Major Costa Ferreira became Minister of Education and for the two short months that this liberal-minded man remained in the Government, I was, as I have already mentioned, his secretary.

Although I held this position for such a short time, from my convenient vantage point in the Minister's office I soon became fully aware of the corrupt practices that the dictatorship had inherited: the numerous officials, for instance, who for years had been receiving a salary without even having an office to go to, or the primary school inspectors who did all their inspecting when the pupils had gone home and the lady teachers were on their own.

The Minister began to change all this but he did not have sufficient time to make much improvement. In my young lieutenant's heart, as in so many others, the idea was taking root that the rottenness of the country could only be remedied by strong men determined to wipe out the ingrained habits of dishonesty and corruption. People were saying that Dr Salazar was such a man and he would see order established. The women were exultant at the thought, I was told by my fiancée, Maria Iva, who today is my dear wife and the mother of my children.

On 14th May 1928 Salazar published the Budget Reform Bill which formulated the principle of combining all revenue and expenditure into one budget. He also began to balance the budget, which had not been done for a century, with the exception of Afonso Costa's attempt in 1912/14. In 1928/29 Salazar presented a balanced budget which caused a furore both at home and abroad.

As a brief indication of his early work, he played a part in the administration of the General Savings Bank, in the Junta of Public Credit, in the contract with the Bank of Portugal and in the circulation of paper money. He also stopped the floating debt, instituted the National Institute of Statistics and established the General Inspection of Finances. He reorganized the Mint, centralized the administration of widows' assistance in the Civil Servants' Benefits Fund and accomplished many other measures in an attempt to create order out of complete chaos. Unfortunately, however, he allowed his liking for order to grow into a soul-destroying obsession, becoming so icily methodical that to look back over his thirty-three years as dictator is enough to make one's blood run cold. Having no personal ties whatsoever, he simply lusted for power and intends to hold on to it as long as he can.

On 5th July 1932 he seized power as Prime Minister with all the prestige of a Messiah. He judged the Army by the type of general with whom he had been in contact. This was the great *volte-face* of the revolution for, having been simply the reorganizer of public finance, he was now the most influential person in the whole of public affairs in Portugal and has remained so for thirty years or more. What a change of role! For many years he held the portfolio for Finance, a subtle means of wielding authority in all spheres of governmental affairs, and ended up by considering himself, and actually becoming, indispensable. The respect accorded to his so-called genius became legendary and later grew into something ridiculous, even imbecile, as I noticed at meetings of high-ranking officials which I attended, although of lower-rank. I was ashamed one day to see admirals and generals restraining their laughter until they had heard the 'bugle-call'— Salazar's own laughter.

I remember when, while still only a major, I was appointed to take charge of the preparations for the disembarkation of British forces in the Azores during the Second World War, and the dictator called a meeting of the high commands as well as the relevant ministers. Salazar, being accustomed to having his subordinates sound him for his opinions before they dared open their mouths, was gradually getting into the habit of holding forth even on technical matters. On one question of air policy, concerning the introduction of ordinary aircraft for the navy, hitherto supplied only with seaplanes, he uttered an opinion which was about twenty years out of date. In the complete silence which followed I, the youngest and least qualified person present, jokingly replied in slang, with apologies for the vulgarism, that His Excellency's idea 'had whiskers on'. Ministers, admirals and generals looked daggers at me and Salazar scowled, perfectly aware that I was not in the habit of using slang, then, perhaps realizing that my words contained a hint of refusal to be mentally cowed, he slowly and feebly raised the left corner of his mouth—Dr Salazar never laughs but even at his most exuberant only smiles. Immediately those present changed their scowls into benevolent glances at this cheeky rascal of a major, and burst into laughter. At this my heart sank: the bemedalled uniforms were no more than lackeys' liveries.

My mission in the Azores during the war

Towards the end of 1941 I was summoned to see the

Minister, Santos Costa, and handed a secret document in English in which the British Government requested information on subjects ranging from the possibility of building aerodromes in the Azores to detailed surveys of ports, highways, medical services, electricity and water supplies and so on. I thrilled with new life at the thought of collaborating in the downfall of the Nazis. I set off for the Azores on 10th December, quickly accomplished my mission, and returned to Lisbon on 8th January 1942, leaving again for London on the 29th. In order to disguise the real purpose of my visit, I was appointed nominal C.O. of half a dozen second-lieutenants who were going for fighter training to Hullavington, near London, and to Paisley, in Scotland, the base of the Torpedo Training Unit.

I handed over my report, known from its blue cover as 'Delgado's Blue Report Number One', to R.A.F. headquarters. As air representative I had as my temporary colleague Wing-Commander Roland Vintras, under the command of the future Air Chief Marshal Sir William Elliot (Intelligence) who, some six years later, when we were equivalent in rank, sat with me on the military committee of N.A.T.O. in Washington. After this, I spent some time working in collaboration with Air Chief Marshal Sir Philip Joubert de la Ferté, head of Coastal Command, whom I was to meet unexpectedly shortly afterwards in the elegant Athenaeum Club in Pall Mall. (Strangely enough, I was made a member of this select club by the delightful secretary, Mr Udal, because some time in my travels I had met and had discussions with Graham, the well known geologist. It was here that I met the eminent scientist, Sir Henry Tizard.)

The R.A.F. knew very little about the Azores and my reconnaissance proved of considerable importance. Thanks to my advice regarding the frequent heavy cloud over the area, they modified their original plans for the proportion of heavy and light anti-aircraft guns defending the aerodromes. Similarly, their intention to use seaplanes was completely changed in view of the information I could give on the sea conditions throughout the year and the awkward high banks of the lakes.

On 19th March 1942 I returned to Lisbon and quickly

set out for the Azores on the 26th, where I supervised the extension of the aerodromes and prepared another enormous report, 'Delgado's Blue Report Number Two', which included an extensive survey and relief maps with contours given to the nearest yard, which I had compiled from photographs. It also covered more easily calculable matters such as water supplies, electrical installations, sewerage and general facilities, Working enthusiastically, I drove my staff hard and managed to return to Portugal by 23rd May, arriving in London on 18th June, where I worked until 25th September, collaborating on the final technical agreements, and then returned to Lisbon.

I wondered whether the Nazis were unaware of all this, for one day I emptied my left-hand pocket, taking out an envelope with thirty-six 100-escudo notes in it, to make room for the documents concerning the technical agreement in connection with our concession of facilities in the Azores. What a tremendous responsibility! When I arrived at my hotel the money which I had put into my outside right-hand pocket had disappeared. Strangely enough a typist in the Portuguese Embassy in London was shortly afterwards arrested as a Nazi spy, being first condemned to death and later reprieved and given a life sentence. Was this a coincidence? I must add that the typist had not touched my papers, for I had typed them myself and sent them direct to Dr Salazar, the War Minister and his Under-Secretary, Santos Costa. Yet no doubt some people were wondering what I, the head of the group of second-lieutenants training in far-distant schools, was doing in London.

From 2nd July to 18th August 1943, I took part in the final political-military discussions in Lisbon, which Air Marshal Madhurst made a special journey to attend, accompanied by Admiral Servaes, Wing-Commander Roland Vintras, whom I have mentioned before, Commander Battini, a naval delegate whom I had already met in the Azores in a civilian capacity, and several others. The Portuguese mission was presided over by Admiral Botelho de Souza. The question arose concerning the defence in territorial waters of the naval convoy bringing the British expeditionary forces, for

Nazi submarines were a great hazard. De Souza objected to having the disembarkation protected by the British, whilst Servães, also of the Portuguese mission, took the opposite view, in face of the Portuguese Navy's inefficiency. The British delegate, red with anger, burst out: 'Admiral, this gentleman is sacrificing an alliance six centuries old for the sake of half a dozen miles of water,' and immediately afterwards left for England. During the lunch break, I hurried to the Under-Secretary for War, without saying a word to de Souza, and managed to settle the matter. Finally, on 18th August 1943, the agreement was signed.

On 9th September I left for London with a combined group of army, naval and air representatives whose purpose was to agree on a plan of Anglo-Portuguese collaboration in order to forestall any German action after the concession of facilities in the Azores was completed. Once again I was aware of the state of friction between an army at war and an army that had been on a peacetime footing for many years and that, moreover, in the mentally devitalizing atmosphere of a dictatorship.

I was extremely ashamed because the Portuguese mission always arrived late, but its chief only censured me for my 'punctuality mania'. It is a difficult business, this struggle between the objective and the subjective, the sense of responsibility conflicting with the fear of the minister back in Lisbon. One day when the others had left the room and I was about to do the same, Colonel Wood, Englishman though he was, gave a resounding kick to a chair, in disgust at the time being wasted in endless reiteration of the same futile topics. I felt very sorry for Brigadier Grant, head of the British delegation, and admired the effort he must have had to make to keep his temper.

On 8th October the British troops disembarked at Angra do Heroísmo, on the Island of Terceira and on the 12th Churchill announced it to the world from the House of Commons, where I sat, overcome with emotion; I shall never forget that moment. On the 30th I returned to Lisbon.

The facilities conceded included the aerodrome at Lajes, on the Island of Terceira, the emergency use of the one at

Santana (Rabo de Peixe), on the Island of São Miguel, as well as freedom to use the ports of Ponta Delgada, on São Miguel, Angra do Heroísmo, on Terceira, and Faial. Lajes possessed the largest runway in the world at that time, 3,280·8 m. (10,600 ft.) by 91·3 m. (300 ft.), and although at first it was only beaten earth, the British and Americans later covered it with steel plate and eventually with asphalt.

This concession meant that a formerly unguarded stretch of the Atlantic could now be patrolled and with a base in the very centre of the area the airmen could use all their fuel for actual patrolling, instead of having to reserve most of it for the return journey as they had had to do when flying from England or Newfoundland. The British activity in the Azores was: 3,115 take-offs, 24,978 flying-hours, 38 submarines detected and 19 attacks, the first submarine being sunk only thirty days after disembarkation.

The agreement of 28th November 1944 made over the base of Santa Maria to the Americans and thus I had a further opportunity of working with those practical-minded people.

After the war, the British Government awarded me the C.B.E. in acknowledgement of my work and in the diploma I was given with the medal, which by the way is one of the finest in my possession since it states the facts clearly instead of being mere vague praise, reference is made to my competence as an officer on the General Staff—and as a politician —pointing out that operations had been started immediately, when everyone in London had thought they would not begin for another six months. It added that I had risked my whole future for the Allied cause, the cause of freedom. I feel very satisfied with what I did, considering that I was an officer serving under a pro-Nazi government. Another happy memory is when, on 14th March 1942, Ambassador Armindo Monteiro summoned me to the Embassy to tell me in the presence of his counsellor, Faria, that His Majesty King George VI had spoken to him about my 'Blue Report Number One' which apparently Churchill had mentioned at one of their weekly luncheons. The general spirit of a democracy is something memorable; nowadays, as Leader of the Opposition, I have to put up with the harshest criticisms from any semi-literate idiot.

In all these missions I worked in close contact with Dr Salazar and, although he deals with paper-work efficiently and capably, he lacks any understanding of human motives, which at times causes him to fall into the most childish errors, such as sensing espionage in every request made by the British. This happened when they wanted to send a radar technician to the Azores and since he did not wish to give permission I had to tell him that the technician would only have access to what was already known through my reports. He had shown annoyance before at the perfectly normal request for an R.A.F. officer to go to the Azores before the actual disembarkation, but fortunately Wing-Commander Vintras, after reading my report, managed to persuade the British High Command to waive their demand, as an exceptional measure.

My work in civil aviation

When the Americans called the Chicago conference in 1944, Salazar was desperate, because we were the only colonial power without an air service to our overseas territories! And so he created the Secretariat of Civil Aviation and appointed me Director-General. We had nothing to work on for, as an American had said, the Portuguese civil airlines consisted of 'one pilot, one plane, one mechanic, one line, once a week to Tangier!' On 31st December 1946 services to Luanda in Angola and Lourenço Marques in Mozambique were started and that very day I asked permission to resign.

It was a difficult task and one small incident will best show how things stood. My second-in-command, at that time Major, now General Humberto Paes, had been chosen by Salazar without my being consulted. I told Salazar then that there was not room for two Humbertos at the head of Civil Aviation but it was a long time before he got round to dismissing him.

I also represented Portugal on the I.C.A.O. (International Civil Aviation Organization) in Canada, and on N.A.T.O.

in Washington. I shall have more to say about my experiences in these international organizations later on, when I describe how my life abroad influenced my revolutionary ideas. Here I shall simply say that in these adventures all over the world I became acquainted with many great people.

My contact with so many varied minds and nationalities was an excellent training-ground for a future democratic candidate for the Presidency of the Republic. Moreover there were the fifty-odd long journeys I made, one of them a complete trip around the world via Australia, when I travelled 53,000 kms. in 198 flying hours; the eight years I spent with permanent international democratic assemblies, and the dozens of international conferences and negotiations for various treaties I attended. All this will give some idea of the exceptional experience I gained in democratic debate and tolerance. It was a profound influence upon my development and it seems that I did have something worthwhile to offer the Opposition when they asked me to be their candidate for the Presidency of the Republic in 1958.

General António Oscar de Fragoso Carmona, President of Portugal 1928–51

Dr Álvaro Lins, Brazilian Ambassador to Lisbon, presenting his credentials at the Palace of Belém, 1957

CHAPTER VII

National wealth and mass poverty

THROUGHOUT its length and breadth, Portugal is a country of beggars crying for bread, work or protection and this not only includes the poor wretches without a penny to their name, but the would-be professor who will never get his chair if P.I.D.E. opposes his nomination, the tradesman who must belong to the appropriate guild if he wishes to sell anything and who will be a failure if there is any suggestion of his possessing unsavoury political views, and even the doctor who needs training in the state hospitals and runs the risk of failing his probationary period if he does not belong to the 'fraternity'.

The situation was analysed a short while ago in *The Reporter* in the U.S.A. The article ended: 'Anyone born Portuguese can only exercise his profession, whatever it might be, subject directly to the political power of the state,' which is only another way of putting what the dictator himself said to a friend of mine: 'They will be just what we want them to be.'

Typical of this outlook is the example of Aquilino Ribeiro, the great writer who, in his seventies, was handed over to the police simply because in his story *Quando os Lobos Uivam* (*When the Wolves Howl*), he criticized the society which Salazar has created and emphasized the stupidity and evil of the totalitarian system.

Misery in Portugal

When studying the human mechanism, it is wise to begin with the fuel it needs to keep it going. The Portuguese exist on a calory intake of some 700 per head less than the minimum as fixed by the F.A.O., but how could it be otherwise with the disgustingly low wages and the notoriously unequal distribution of wealth which earns a farm-labourer in Alentejo 16 escudos a day for the few days in the week when he can manage to find employment?

To avoid being accused of the common political tactic which I wholeheartedly condemn, of giving a dismal picture and refusing any credit to one's opponents, merely in order to support one's own argument, I shall simply quote the comments of the Minister of Economics, Vieira Barbosa, who confirms that the average cost of 1,000 calories increased from 1·43 escudos to 3·48 between 1938 and 1948. From this he concluded that taking the basis of a modest ration of 5,000 calories per family, and comparing the salaries sufficient to buy enough food in 1938, a worker who was employed for the whole of 1958 would not have been able to feed a family on the average daily wage of 20 escudos, but would have had a 2% deficit.

When, however, in 1958 my electoral campaign took me through Alentejo, weeping women clung to me to tell me that during the past winter they had been earning 8 escudos a day and even then for only part of the week. One could see the proof of their words in the children who surrounded me, for they were all skin and bone with large sad eyes which could not fail to compel anyone to give them a crust of bread.

However little I like politics, especially among the Latins who on the whole are badly educated and far from responsible in public affairs, this sad picture imposes a personal obligation to remain in politics until there is some genuine organization to ensure that there are no more of those heart-rending little faces with their mournful eyes.

My Brazilian secretary, Sra Arajaryr Campos, told me that she had had a young Portuguese maid who had come over as an emigrant and had told her that in Portugal she had never eaten meat, but could now enjoy good-sized steaks at her employer's house.

This hungry girl had touched on a very important point, for the annual consumption of meat in Portugal is in fact

15 kilos a head against 69 kilos in the U.S.A., 61 in England and 43 in West Germany. As for milk, the Portuguese drink 1 litre a month in contrast to 20 to 40 litres in less backward countries.

This proves that the fundamental proteins are a luxury for the poor and middle classes. You have only to look at the country people to see how they soon became mere bags of bones; the women between forty and fifty age at an unnatural rate and the men grow bent and bow-legged, while both sexes soon lose all their teeth. The lack of vitamins produces either scrawniness or, through too many carbohydrates, the sickly, bloated type.

Cleverly, though with painful accuracy, the facts of protein consumption in Portugal have been described as: 'One small glass of milk a day, one steak a week, three eggs a month and a chicken a year.' Considering that so many people have three eggs a day and a proportionate amount of the other food it is not surprising that, as I have seen myself, there are many both in the country and in the city who never taste this sort of food except on feast days. In the country they do not eat eggs or chicken for, since their income is barely enough to live on, it is only by selling these little extras that they can buy anything beyond the basic needs for sleeping, eating and reproducing. Yet the Portuguese worker spends between 67 and 87% of his income on food and, in consequence, lives little better than an animal. If we compare this to a semi-socialist country of the progressive democratic type such as Sweden, we find that there only 31% of the family budget is spent on food. To take France as an example, the most politically mature and socially progressive of the Latin countries, we see that 49% of the income is used for the same purpose.

Salaries

A salary can only be estimated in relation to the amount it buys, as I remember clearly from the statistics I learnt over five years ago when I matriculated at the American University of Washington, although I was no more than a dabbler in this subject, interested in learning just a little about economics. An American labourer worked fifty hours to buy a cotton shirt, a suit and a pair of shoes, while a Russian labourer had to work five times as long. This tells us far more than any simple statement of roubles and dollars, which would give no worthwhile information about their respective buying powers.

A similar analysis of the situation in Portugal gives alarming results. It is difficult to calculate the farm-worker's wage, for there is widespread unemployment, but it probably amounts to about two-thirds of the average industrial worker's which is about 24 escudos. A comparison of the latter's income shows that in order to buy a kilo of meat, he must work almost a full day of some 6 or 7 hours in contrast to $1\frac{1}{2}$ hours in England. As for milk, an Englishman needs to work only a quarter of an hour for the price of a litre, while the Portuguese labourer, who never drinks it anyhow, would have to work four times as long. A kilo of potatoes, one of the ingredients of 'caldo verde' (green broth) which is the staple diet among the under-nourished northerners, requires nearly an hour of the Portuguese labourer's time, against five minutes in America. What can he do if he has a family to feed, especially since one kilo of bread, the basic food in Portugal, also costs an hour's wage?

This goes to prove that the nutritional standard of the Portuguese is comparable to that of a Tunisian or Congolese as the *New Scientist* pointed out on 21st July 1960. Wages which have dropped by nearly a third between 1938 and 1958 can only buy hunger and thus, since there is no bread, the only luxuries possible are Salazar's equivalent to the Roman circuses—football, fado and Fatima. (The fado is a melancholy national song and Fatima is a town where Our Lady is supposed to have appeared in 1917.)

The Health Problem

A Portuguese is actually born in unusual circumstances, for there are many villages where it is unheard of to have a midwife or doctor present and as many as 50% of the mothers deliver their babies without any help.

The mortality rate during the first year is 88 per 1,000,

against an average of 50 per 1,000 in 102 other countries. During Salazar's reign the position in relation to Czechoslovakia, Japan and Singapore has, oddly enough, been reversed, for in these three countries the rate in 1925 was double that of Portugal whilst now it is the other way round. (W.H.O. Epidemiological and Vital Statistics Report.)

Even if the Portuguese does not die at birth it is almost impossible for him to get medical attention, since in most cases he has to choose between eating and receiving treatment and even when this is available it is often too expensive for him, leaving him no alternative but death. In Portugal there is only 1 doctor per 1,400 inhabitants as against 1 per 800 in Italy; similarly there is one nurse per 3,000 inhabitants in contrast to 1 per 500 in the western democracies. The consequences are inevitable and mean that 58 persons per 1,000 die of tuberculosis in contrast to 5 per 1,000 in Holland, and for every child that dies of whooping-cough in England there are four in Portugal, whilst the ratio for measles in these two countries is 1 to 9.

Housing and Public Assistance

Supposing a Portuguese manages to survive all this and in order to get married wants to buy a house. The figures from the last census show that out of a total of 2,047,398 families 2,592 had no accommodation, 10,596 lived in temporary buildings, 2,583 in dwellings unfit for habitation and 193,221 shared a house. From facts I have received from people living in the country, I can assure the reader that these official statistics are a big understatement.

You cannot read by electric light or listen to the radio because, as I found when I spent the summer in Cela, there is no electricity in spite of the promises made a dozen or more years ago. When at last it was going to be installed, I visited the town as candidate for the Presidency and then the President of the Alcobaca Town Council, the municipality to which Cela belongs, informed the poor wretches living there that by giving me such an enthusiastic welcome they had forfeited the right to this luxury. Of the 3,374 parishes in Portugal, only 1,251 had electricity in 1953, of which 484 already had it in 1935, showing an increase of a mere 42 parishes a year.

Moreover, even in a general's house the excessive cost of electricity entails a constant need to economize on the lighting and heating, and this was one of the most disagreeable contrasts I noticed when returning to Lisbon from my mission in Washington. The consumption per head is approximately 250 kw. per year while in Switzerland it is 2,000 kw. and in Norway 5,000 kw.

When he reaches old age and can no longer work, the Portuguese with no means of livelihood must either depend upon his children or, as happens in the majority of cases, end up by living on charity because public assistance and old age pensions are rarely more than theoretical benefits.

The situation in regard to Portuguese national assistance shows just how badly the country needs new blood and new ideas. Although it pays far less it extorts from both employee and employer far more than is paid in any other European country; with the 7% from the employee and 18% from the employer a total of 25% is contributed to National Insurance in contrast to 5·3% in England, 18·66% in Germany and 18% in Spain.

When I returned from Canada I met one of my old servants, well on in years now, who asked me if I could try to get her a small allowance from the National Assistance. At that time I was not yet under any real suspicion, even if I was beginning to be considered as an old '*grognard*', and so the Director-General of National Assistance received me kindly. In a most open-handed manner he granted the poor soul a subsistence allowance of 90 escudos a month, which is just enough to rent a small, windowless attic with nothing left over for food, clothing and so on. Yet this was the most that the influence of a highly respected colonel, who had just returned from an important mission abroad, could obtain!

It is not surprising that in the period 1948/53, the Portuguese had an average life expectation of 49 years in comparison with 71 in Sweden, 69 in Holland and 68 in England.

National Income

Having discussed the individual point of view I should like

to describe the more general situation. The worker alone has no rights and even his union is no more than a small cog in the totalitarian wheel. He cannot vote or make any choice and hardly dares express his views, and thus it is not surprising that only 40% of the turnover in industry is paid out in wages, leaving 60% as capital profits in contrast with 70% and 30% respectively in the more advanced, democratic countries—there is no Keynes or Marx in Portugal.

Neither is it astonishing that because of this almost medieval stagnation, the country's income per head is no more than 182 dollars, against 1,453 dollars in the U.S.A., 342 in Argentina and 209 in Turkey and this in spite of its good sources of raw materials in the colonies which are at least 23 times as large as their mother-country.

As many readers will probably be unfamiliar with economics it is best to define the terms 'national product' and 'national income by factor costs'. According to the U.N. definition 'national income by factor costs' is the total sum of all individual incomes obtained in the production of goods and services over the length of a year. Thus, it comprises all salaries, including national assistance, rents, dividends, and interests and profits of self-employed persons, as well as company profits before payment of taxes and the net incomes payable to other countries.

'Gross national product by factor costs' means the national income by factor costs plus any firm's reserves to cover depreciation, maintenance costs and irrecoverable debts.

The 1958 Report of the Finance Minister, Pinto Barbosa, contains the following details on the National Gross Product:

(in 1,000 contos—1 conto being 1,000 escudos)

Sectors of Activity	1957 (Current Prices)
1. Agriculture, forestry and fishing . . .	14,977
2. Industry	19,355
3. Electrical energy and services . . .	18,834
4. Internal Gross Product by factor costs . .	53,216
5. Net income from abroad	87
6. Gross National Product by factor costs . .	53,303

Seeing that forestry and fishing represent $\frac{1}{6}$ of the first sector of activity, agriculture must comprise a very small percentage of the national product. Since half the population of 8 million inhabitants work in agriculture, forestry and fishing, their annual product per head appears to be a little under 3,800 escudos. The average for the other half of the population employed in industry and services rises to something like 9,600 escudos, much more than double, which is obviously a serious disparity to which I shall return later.

When discussing the national product at the market price of 1954, Dr Francisco Moura, Professor of Economics who, to judge by his position, cannot be exactly inimical to Dr Salazar, produced the following figures, making allowance for monetary fluctuations:

$$1947 \quad . \quad . \quad 37\cdot8 \text{ million contos}$$
$$1956 \quad . \quad . \quad 53\cdot4 \quad \text{,,} \quad \text{,,}$$

This shows an increase of 42% or a cumulative rate of +4%.

To sum up our economic progress we can say that, allowing for the annual population growth of 1% over this period, the national product per head is increasing at the rate of approximately 3% per annum.

It is worth repeating at this point the statement made during my electoral campaign in 1958 by my friend, Cunha Leal, the Opposition Leader in the Parliament preceding the military dictatorship and one of the most brilliant minds in the country:

'If we were to maintain the rate of increase in national product of the ten years ending in 1960, and if the American rate were to decrease by 2%, it would take us no less than a century to reach a quarter of the North American average. If, on the other hand, the national revenue of the U.S.A. and the O.E.E.C. countries were to remain static at their present rate, while ours increased at the annual rate of 3% a head, we should need eighty years to reach the United States level and forty years to attain that of the O.E.E.C. countries.'

It has needed thirty years of static peace and order to increase the prestige of the escudo, by linking it with other strong currencies such as the dollar or the Swiss franc. Yet they do not realize that there is no point in having enormous uninvested deposits and bank dividends, for it is only by keeping money in circulation that more can be made. You can still see 100-escudo notes which, although minted years ago, can be stood upright on the table when folded proving that they have never been in circulation. Thus, paradoxically, this poor country still possesses great wealth, but it is all concentrated in the hands of some fifty families.

Small wonder then that in the Common Market or the European Free Trade Association, Portugal always appears severely restricted and begging humbly for indulgence.

Salazar and Stagnation

The iron discipline of the Portuguese Corporative Organization with a budget of millions of contos also displays this same opposition to progress and thus acts as a burden on the consumer and provides a good shelter for the inept and the inapt; through its activities, Portuguese products are gradually being excluded from the world markets. To take Port wine as an example; anyone who has travelled abroad must have realized that the demand for sherry and gin is growing, and whisky is now being distributed throughout the world. The growing taste for dry wines and liqueurs suggests that Port should be adapted to these new circumstances by being transformed from the high-quality digestive it is today into an apéritif more acceptable to modern taste. Yet this aristocratic wine from the banks of the Douro, where each vine only yields a bare half-dozen bunches of grapes, should never be degraded to the point of being sold as I saw in New York at 1·25 dollars a bottle, the same price as Californian white wine. When I discussed this with Salazar one day, he replied that I was a pilot not a merchant, but I have drunk and bought Port in countries all over the world, while he had had it only in Portugal, so I should know more about it.

Worse still, when I was in Washington I tried to open six sample bottles of Port but as soon as I put the cork-screw in, the corks crumbled. I was told that the corks were of such bad quality because they tried to save half a tostão on each, a coin of so little value that it is no longer in circulation. The Americans must have a very poor opinion of an organization which allows such things.

Again in Washington I noticed the same thing happening with our sardines which are undoubtedly the best in the world. When I inquired why American housewives were so reluctant to buy them I discovered that it was because the tins were difficult to open.

Finally, in Canada I saw chestnuts on sale and hurried to buy some. I patriotically remarked 'They're Portuguese, aren't they?' but the shopkeeper indignantly replied that he would never buy Portuguese chestnuts again, for the three times he had stocked them they had been maggoty.

As Jean Darcet said in an article in *Prospectiva* in January 1959: 'The monetary stability which benefits countries like Portugal is counter-balanced by a certain economic and social stagnation which favours neither the power of the state nor the people's standard of living.' This point was also touched upon in a publication by the economic branch of N.A.T.O., which I saw in Washington. This was in reply to the complaints of the Portuguese Government which, in the event of a war with Russia, would be unable to send soldiers beyond the Pyrenees, even though it spends 32% of its revenue on the Armed Forces, against a bare 9% on education, although half the country still remains illiterate, and only 4% on public assistance.

I shall end this chapter with a short personal story. Although she was only seventeen in 1958, my daughter, Iva Humberta, devoted herself wholeheartedly to anonymous acts of charity. She would get hold of old clothes and distribute them to the poor wretches in Pedreira do Hilário, one of the shanty towns in the Alcântara district of Lisbon. One day she took me with her and I came away so horrified that when I got home I immediately had to have a bath to disinfect myself. One 'house' there had no walls at all and its roof was simply a horizontal rock jutting out of the quarry. Another hut had a doorway only 1·4 m. high and inside was an 8 hours-old child whom its mother had left in order to return to work outside.

CHAPTER VIII

My work abroad and how I became candidate for the Opposition

I HAVE been asked more than once exactly when I decided to devote my life to overthrowing the dictatorship. The first point to bear in mind is that if a general is held in such slight regard in Portugal today, you can imagine the position of a major or captain, especially when he is not in command of any troops as I was not for most of my career. Nevertheless it is worth remarking that, as a lieutenant-colonel and Director-General of Civil Aviation in 1945, I immediately caused trouble when I came across some men armed with brush and ladder who were about to stick some electoral propaganda for the National Union, the only real party, on the walls of a public building. I forbade them to do so, saying that it was a State establishment but all the same people soon began to talk. It was about this time that the National Unionists wrote to me asking me to join their ranks and pay the appropriate fees. I answered that if I had to join their party in order to be Director-General I would rather resign, for I was not going to allow myself to be tied down.

Therefore, instead of trying to find an exact date it would be better to give a few sketches of my life abroad where I was able to compare the methods of the various governments and the relations between individuals.

P.I.C.A.O. and I.C.A.O.

In December 1946 I had resigned as Director-General of

Civil Aviation, but a month later I was on my way to Australia as head of the Portuguese delegation to the regional conference of the South Pacific which includes the Portuguese colony of Timor. While still Director-General, I had suggested that for the sake of economy and considering how unimportant Timor was no one should be sent from the metropolis, especially as there were few people available for such a trip. However, Salazar disagreed and as I was no longer in Civil Aviation I could not argue that I had no time to go. The dictator had the idea that because Timor had been invaded by the Japanese and Australians during the Second World War it was advisable both from the political and diplomatic points of view that our delegation should be a 'presentable one'. Strangely enough, the only part that the Minister of Communications, Engineer Cancela de Abreu, actually played in this affair was to settle the small matter of travelling expenses, for it was the dictator who was really in charge. As head of the mission I had to be prepared to make certain minimal compromises involving financial as well as technical matters; for example, whether we would undertake to build an international airport. Dr Salazar would give no decisive answer to this but politely referred to my world-wide experience and said that I would see when I got there which, of course, was all done for the sake of form.

Naturally, in order to give the Portuguese delegation the politico-diplomatic gloss that Salazar expected, I had to rely upon my inherent administrative abilities and wide variety of experience—for the 'encyclopaedic' is someone who knows a little about a lot of things. I succeeded on this mission and I would like to quote verbatim from a short note I made at that time: 'Salazar wrote to me commending my work and, quite unsolicited, ordered me to be paid 2,000 escudos for personal expenses.'

I arrived back from the Antipodes after a complete tour around the world, travelling outwards via the Mediterranean and Indian Sea and back over the Pacific and Atlantic, thus gaining an extra day on 10th March when I crossed the International Date Line. I seemed to have become a sort of Ambassador of the Air for immediately on my return the new Minister of Communications, Gomes de Araújo, who has since been promoted general, invited me to set off on a new mission for the Air Force, by taking part in the Euro-Mediterranean conference of P.I.C.A.O. (Provisional International Civil Aviation Organization) in Paris. I left on 12th April and returned on the 29th, when, after only one day's rest, I set out for Montreal where the general conference of P.I.C.A.O. was being held—it was at this meeting that the provisional organization became definitely known as I.C.A.O.

To give some idea of how I had to work at this period of my life, which was always extremely busy through lack of time and too many orders from my superiors, let me quote an extract from my notes: 'I had meetings today with Salazar, the Colonial Minister, the Minister for Foreign Affairs and the Minister of Communications.'

Although Salazar acknowledged my experience on international committees, he still insisted upon maintaining the façade, the smooth, artificial surface hiding the sordid truth, and so he appointed an ambassador named Bianchi as head of the mission to the Aeronautic Assembly in Washington. This was a great mistake, for the other delegates sensed immediately that Portugal, the poor relation of world aviation, was only thinking of her political position, intending to hinder the progress in serious and mutually advantageous matters such as the construction of aerodromes, the organization of radio systems to help navigation and granting of better facilities for commercial aircraft over Portuguese territories.

Referring to the preliminaries of the conference, I had regretfully to report on 8th May 1947 that Portugal had not been elected to any committee whatsoever. Naturally, members of the Air Forces are not at all keen on having to work with ambassadors like Bianchi, however pleasant they might be, for they speak a completely different language. They do not share the same outlook and the service-men cannot feel that warmth towards them which they feel for their fellows who have faced the same dangers and shared those awful moments when land and air are indistinguishable in thick mist and the radio breaks down.

Salazar had appointed Bianchi because he was anxious to

keep up appearances and his only concern was that Portugal should be elected a member of the I.C.A.O. Council; why, I simply could not understand. It is a characteristic defect of intelligent men like Salazar that when they do not travel and are unrestrained by any opposition, they begin to show signs of living in a fantasy world, where newspaper accounts of diplomatic successes take the place of fairies, and their terse pronouncements to interviewers, at which they imagine the whole world trembles, act as witches' curses. This was the case with the dictator when he used to tell me that he was just as good as any other ruler or shout remarks such as 'I *warned* Europe', as if the other countries could hear him.

As I have said, the début of the Portuguese delegation in Montreal was not exactly brilliant. Thus on 18th May I had an interview with the *Gazette* at Bianchi's request in which I emphasized Portugal's importance in world aviation, without of course mentioning that it was only five months earlier, and then only after much effort on my part, that the first air service to the colonies had been started.

At last, on the 22nd, the great day arrived when Portugal was elected to the Council of the 21 countries. The delegation was jubilant but I was a pilot and was not so much concerned with the political façade as with helping to furnish the world with what the Convention described as 'a safe, regular, efficient and economical air service'. The next day I put forward a proposal which was to provide the main controversy of the conference. This was the technical system of units for ground-air communication, now given in the I.C.A.O. Table Unit, which is the table of standards to which all nations must conform.

It was a fierce battle but the French and Brazilian delegations were a great help to me as were I.A.T.A. (International Air Transport Association), although they themselves had no vote. In the technical committee the result was sixteen in favour, three abstentions and one against: the sole opposers were the British group.

Only the decision of the General Assembly was needed now, but Bianchi was being cajoled by the U.S.A. delegation and he hovered around me, trying to convince me how disagreeable it would be to be on bad terms with America. I stood firm, but naturally I was depressed and embarrassed at having to defend my own proposal against the Portuguese delegation.

On the 26th the U.S.A. objected to my proposal on a legal basis, claiming that under Paragraph '1' of Article 54 of the International Agreement of 28th February 1945, it was not within the power of the Assembly to establish 'Standards and Recommended Practices'. I went onto the platform and destroyed this argument, emphasizing that 'those who wield great power can wield it in favour of small things' and '*quos abundat non nocet*'. The result was eighteen votes in favour and seven against.

When the conference ended on the 28th the other members of the delegation were somewhat cool at our success, but I shrugged this off. However, Bianchi did eventually do me justice in his report and so all ended well. Yet in all my later contacts with the Ministry of Foreign Affairs I was still aware of the diplomats' antagonism towards me, since I had spent nine years on advanced flying courses which was far more than they had done. Moreover I never gaped with admiration when any of them chose to play the sage and acted as if he had been entrusted with some valuable secret, simply in order to win my support for something with which I could not agree. This was one of the great lessons I learnt regarding a totalitarian régime's method of conducting international politics.

I returned to Lisbon and then a few days later returned to Canada where I had been appointed Portuguese representative in the I.C.A.O. Council. While I had been away, my place had been taken by Caldeira Queiroz who was at that time Minister at the Embassy and a member of the delegation to the Assembly, which was why he had remained in Montreal. Things were not made very easy for me when I arrived. I found no furniture, typewriter, paper or even money to buy anything but had to start completely from scratch. There was no chance of money being sent from Lisbon so, desperately, I bought the minimum of furniture on credit. This was just another example of the dictator's methods: everything possible had been done to get the country elected but now that that had been managed, it did not matter how embarrassing our position was, for the major objective had been the transatlantic telegram announcing that we had succeeded.

I spent three years in Montreal and found it a hard life representing a very backward country which in the words of the great Plessman of K.L.M., 'neither does anything itself nor lets anything be done'. However, I saved our reputation by leaving a good name and close friends behind me, for I was always ready to co-operate in anything that a member of the Council could do to further our work, even if at times this meant going beyond my instructions. Portugal was one of the most recalcitrant of countries to concede aerial rights, which are essential in order to give commercial aircraft the same status as ships, since the doctrine of *mare clausum* was replaced by *mare librum* and all that this entailed.

In N.A.T.O. An Interlude in Lisbon

I returned to Lisbon in order to spend a year commanding troops and also to take the High Command course, the two prerequisites for promotion to the higher ranks: in the first I received two credits and in the second was classified as 'very competent'. Although unaware of it, I was acquiring the assets which, six years later, would influence the Opposition to invite me to be their candidate for the Presidency of the Republic.

At the end of 1952 I left for Washington and, although still only a colonel, I had to work with twelve others who were either generals or admirals representing their countries on the Military Committee in N.A.T.O. and, moreover, for a time I also had to act as Military and Air Attaché. As in Canada, I found it a hard life, for Portugal had less troops than any other European country with the exception of Luxembourg. Even though I have been discharged from the Air Force, my principles and sense of responsibility will not permit me to mention even now various matters which passed through my hands as head of the N.A.T.O. mission.

The growing revolt

On 18th May 1956, while I was still in Washington, I

General Craveiro Lopes,
President of Portugal 1951–8

Colonel F. Santos Costa, former Portuguese Minister of
Defence, at a N.A.T.O.
meeting in Paris, April 1958

General Delgado (left) and Captain Henrique Galvăo photographed
together in Caracas, October 1959

received a letter and knew only too well who had written it although it was not signed. I was asked to return to Lisbon 'to organize a movement', but because the Government did not want me in Portugal they made me stay in America longer than anyone was allowed by law to remain on a mission abroad. When I asked for permission to return to Lisbon on 26th August 1956 it was refused. However, I did get to Portugal by obtaining a special permit to deal with my personal affairs, and once there I contacted Major 'R' on 1st November to make the arrangements for a revolt which was to take place when I managed to get out of my post in Washington.

Meanwhile I made a couple of visits to Henrique Galvão who was in prison, and on the last one he asked me to get him a revolver which I actually managed to pass on to an intermediary before I left. However, although I had wrapped up the weapon to make it look like a book, I could not disguise its weight and so he became suspicious and opened the parcel. When he found what it contained he decided not to give it to Galvão. I shall not bother to describe the outcry when it came out that I, the head of the delegation to N.A.T.O., had visited Galvão, a political prisoner, especially since I was the only officer on active service in sympathy with his views.

My special leave came to an end on the 23rd and I had to return to Washington, paying all travelling expenses myself. When eventually I managed to get back to Portugal in September 1957, I was given no military command, either because I was under suspicion or else genuinely unpopular. I went back to my post as Director-General of Civil Aviation.

Rui Luís Gomes was proposed for the Presidency of the Republic but rejected by the Council of State in 1949 and dismissed from his Chair of Mathematics for political reasons: he is now in Argentina in the Chair of Mathematical Physics in the University of Baía Branca. I had the opportunity of meeting him in Lisbon during a visit he made in 1958 and remember him as someone full of hope for better times to come. His photograph appeared all over the world, showing his face and head bandaged after the police, who respect no one, had violently ill-treated him during a political meeting. (As I write this the same police have just been beating up Artur Andrade, the architect, and a leader of the 'third force', to whom I am very closely attached because he was my General Secretary during the elections.)

Norton de Matos, the Grand Master of the Freemasons, aroused the country from its lethargy, even though it was predominantly Catholic, and this warned the dictator in no uncertain terms of its hostility towards the régime, for it had endured his deadening discipline for too long. However, as he had no guarantee of freedom, Norton stood down from the candidature. During his campaign the Communist Party seriously prejudiced his chances, as did someone else who suddenly appeared on the scene and introduced an obscurantist note into the propaganda by discussing religious dogmas such as the Immaculate Conception. This was a throwback to the sort of tactics which had preceded the setting up of the Republic in 1910 and which in these days is a subject of ridicule for the progressive democratic countries.

Norton de Matos was a cultured, energetic person but throughout his life he was constantly criticized and, I might add, I myself followed the general example and, until I was about thirty, censured his actions in Africa. Now, after his death, I have changed my opinion. I must confess that I was taken by surprise during my visit to Angola in 1938 when my chauffeur replied to my remarks about various things I had noticed by saying: 'It's quite simple. If you see anything worthwhile you can be sure it was Norton's work.'

On 18th April 1951 General Carmona died, after twenty-three years of carrying out the non-existent duties of Head of State. A short while before, on 25th January, General Eduardo da Costa Ferreira had also passed away; he was defence counsel during my court-martial, as I have already mentioned. On account of his liberal-mindedness, his culture and intelligence, he was, of all the officers in the Army, the one most likely to be chosen as candidate for the Opposition. Several had in fact considered him as such but when the actual candidate, Admiral Quintão Meireles, was chosen, very few knew him. At the beginning of the dictatorship this admiral had, despite his low rank, risen to become Minister of Foreign Affairs in a period of constant ministerial changes.

I had returned from Canada in order to fulfil the conditions of my promotion to general and, although I was acting as Procurator in the National Defence Department of the Corporative Chamber, I had little to do with politics. This position meant that I had to judge the usefulness of the military regulations before they went before the National Assembly (the political chamber) and thus I had the right, a very unusual one indeed, of pruning the proposed laws of the Ministers.

On the death of Carmona, the ex-Minister and President of the Corporative Chamber asked me to deliver the eulogy at his funeral but I begged to be excused. However he insisted and, not knowing what to say about someone who had had such an uninteresting career, I composed a few words about 'the heroism of inaction', for that had been his life. He had worn a sword that he never unsheathed and, if at official ceremonies he had stood in front of Salazar, in all other matters the dictator always had the lead.

Meireles's rival was Craveiro Lopes who was chosen simply because Salazar wanted a general as President. When I was invited to speak on behalf of Craveiro Lopes, I declined on the grounds that this was contrary to military regulations, but those who had asked me assured me that there would be no obstacles in that direction. When I was due to speak, however, the chairman handed me a note to say that my speech would be omitted because of lack of time. This was not the real reason, for when I came in I had quietly distributed to the press a summary of what I intended to say about corruption in the country. This, therefore, was why I was not allowed to speak.

In July 1952 Henrique Galvão was in prison accused of conspiring against the Government and I decided to pay him a visit, even though we were little more than acquaintances, having only spoken to each other some dozen times in the twenty-six years since the '28th May'. I was indignant at the way a soldier of that period was being treated and offered to act as witness in his defence, but he refused on the grounds that it would deprive me of my stars, for I was still a colonel then.

Three months later I set off on a lengthy mission to Washington and from then on we corresponded in spite of difficulties. Whenever I returned to Europe I visited him and this naturally gave rise to talk and made P.I.D.E. annoyed, although they did not have the courage to refuse permission. Although we had been friends for so short a time, I was the only officer on the active list who went to see him and visits from those on the reserve were few and far between.

I have already mentioned in an earlier chapter how in November 1956 I became deeply involved in a military and civilian conspiracy, when I came back to Lisbon after the Government had refused permission for me to end my period of duty in Washington, which I had requested in August. I made the journey at my own expense and told Henrique Galvão what I was planning to do. The next year he wrote to me in Washington saying that he had found a simple way to bring about the downfall of Salazar but, in spite of the fact that the letter would not be opened by P.I.D.E., he did not state how this could be done. About the same time I also received a letter from an officer asking me to return and lead the revolt. This goes to show the optimism of the Portuguese! Finally, I managed to get out of Washington after being there for five years, although the law stipulates that a mission abroad can only last three or, in exceptional cases, four years. As there was no military command vacant I was appointed Director-General of Civil Aviation for the second time, having been given that position before on 1st October 1957. On Friday, 25th, I visited Henrique Galvão and found that his method for deposing Salazar was for me to stand as candidate for the Presidency. I had to think this over and arranged that on the Monday I would send him a letter and if my signature was underlined, it would be the signal for him to write to his friends to tell them about the idea. I agreed with his plan and sent out word of it.

Galvão wrote to António Sérgio, a well-known member of the Opposition, and sent the letter through Dr Sebastião

Ribeiro, who was to act as my lawyer during my candidature. He carried it to Oporto without knowing what it contained, but since his mind was occupied with the fact that P.I.D.E. was on his track because of an article he had published, he left the letter in his case in the hotel and did not think of it until much later. Consequently, it did not reach António Sérgio in time to be of any use.

On 1st November, Major 'R', whom I have already mentioned when describing the preliminaries of the 1956 revolt, visited me and told me that rumours were going around that I was going to stand as a candidate. This was the second channel through which the idea reached me.

On the 14th, António Sérgio came to see me and asked whether I was willing to have my name put forward. When I told him that I had been expecting him he replied that he had heard nothing from Henrique Galvão. So, through yet another channel, and this time a more important one, my candidature was growing more definite. Meanwhile I continued to plan the military revolt.

On 4th January 1958 Artur Andrade, the architect, accompanied by Dr Rodrigo de Abreu, a nephew of the writer of the same name, visited me at my office in Civil Aviation and proposed that I should stand as candidate. After the 'third force', the people of Oporto, had decided to make their own choice, a period of inaction followed, for the old members of the 'classic opposition', the 'Directory', which I have already described, could not make up their mind, firstly, as to whether they should put up a candidate and, secondly, as to whom they should choose if they did. They had thought of supporting Meireles against me and some had even suggested Professor Azevedo Gomes. Admiral Cabeçadas informed me of their vacillation after having discussed it with Henrique Galvão who had stated that I would not mind 'abdicating' in favour of Meireles. He had made this decision without asking my opinion but counted upon the friendship which had grown out of my visits to him in prison.

However, this indecision had begun to irritate me and so, when Cabeçadas came to see me to make a last effort, I replied that I should remain a candidate, nominated by sponsors in

Oporto, with or without the support of the Directory and with or without Meireles.

In two secret, vital meetings in Oporto on 19th January and 1st March, my candidature was settled. At the second meeting I had to make my intentions clear, for there was an idea that I should announce that under certain conditions I should retain the present government, including Dr Salazar. I rejected such a propsoal out of hand saying that if they insisted upon it I should leave for Lisbon and they would have to find another candidate. They left out this condition, which had obviously been included through over-cleverness, for it would give rise to a completely opposite situation to the one they expected.

During these negotiations my official and conspiratorial life continued apace. I was sent to France and Geneva for meetings of various aviation committees. I dashed from Lisbon to the Azores and the Cape Verde Islands and on 29th April went to see some friends in Madrid. I stayed at the Palace Hotel and the police did not even allow me any peace there until eventually I called the manager and told him that I would leave immediately if my telephone continued to be tapped.

By 15th April the secret could be kept no longer and the *Diário de Lisboa* announced my name as candidate. Then at last the *Diário de Notícias*, the largest paper, shamefacedly slipped in a tiny paragraph on the second page: obviously the name of the Opposition candidate seemed to be of little interest to the nation, even though he was a contributor to the paper. Curiously enough, and in contrast to this, the *New York Times* of 10th April 1958 wrote a long article about me and published a photograph.

On the 17th I informed the Minister of Communications and sent in an official request for details of my obligations as a soldier, since Dr Salazar, never thinking for one moment that an officer on active service would stand as candidate for the Opposition, had left the law obscure on this point. In this request I also asked when my special leave would begin, for this was an undisputed right in more progressive countries. Annoyed, Salazar replied that in regard to the first point the obligations of a candidate were the concern of the Supreme Court of Justice, not his and, as for the second, he would give no leave whatsoever. This meant that if I had not had thirty days' leave due to me I should probably not have been able to stand.

The fierce campaign against me was beginning, but I was determined to brave a government that was so strong and yet so weak that the censor had to cut out the advance notice of my return from Madrid. My own campaign opened on 10th May, but I decided that before then I would issue my historic 'Proclamation to the Portuguese People'. This was a lengthy document outlining my programme and showing the basis of agreement between the anti-totalitarian forces.

CHAPTER IX

Prelude and pre-election tricks

WE lost the election long before polling-day. First of all, it is nothing but a fraud to hold elections when no opposition party is allowed to exist. Many foreign democrats cannot understand this pre-election trickery, either because they are uninformed, unintelligent, or too naïve, and it is quite futile to try to explain it to them. It is impossible to organize a political front in the thirty days of semi-liberty which are generously conceded every seven years.

Even if it were possible there is another obstacle. The electoral rolls are disgracefully falsified so that a large number of voters who are suspected of anti-Salazarist feelings are struck off and many others are left out, so much so, indeed, that I am told that in Angola some 40% do not appear on the lists at all. I shall not bother to discuss the possibility of amending these lists by legal action for that is quite out of the question.

Supposing, however, that we could win, even in these circumstances, we would still be confronted by yet another obstacle. Copies are made of the electoral lists and these are essential, under the Portuguese system, for they supply the political organizations with the names and addresses of the electors and these receive their voting papers at home, either through the post or by hand.

The National Union, the only legal party, receives a copy of these lists and the distribution of papers is made easy for them since, apart from all the normal facilities of an unprohibited party, with headquarters, subscriptions and officials, they are also given help by the Government to allow them even to use the policemen as errand-boys to take the papers to the voters. On 11th April I protested to the Minister of the Interior, Dr Trigo Negreiros, against the difficulties the Opposition has in getting a copy of the lists. He sent me the following reply in a letter on the 24th: 'This ministry has no copies of the electoral rolls at its disposal and cannot therefore satisfy the request of the candidate for the Presidency of the Republic.' They did not openly oppose the candidate but, more subtly, stifled him. We were not allowed photostats or even typed copies to be made of the rolls but only hand-written ones. Thus there would not be enough time to obtain a copy and moreover, without a photostat, the Opposition could not prove that even more names were not being struck off before polling-day. Yet, since it was just possible that the Government might lose, even using these methods, a few trustworthy legionnaires would begin to queue up early in the morning, pretending that they wanted to copy out the lists from the single original. Obviously the Opposition members would have no chance.

The fourth obstacle was the manner by which the Government broke their promise of freedom of the press. The baseness of the Salazarist government is proved by the following small incident. A major in the Air Force, Joaquim Baltazar, decided to take part in the so-called 'campaign of redress' which was aroused by my having announced that if I were ever elected I should not keep Dr Salazar in the Government. Here is the Major's telegram, published on 14th May 1958:

'As a combatant in the revolts of 18th April, 19th June, 28th May and 7th February, I should like to protest and express my regret for the insult directed at Your Excellency and, through you, to the Nation to which I offer my humble services and even my life, by sending my respects to Your Excellency and praying God that He grant you many more years of life and good health, so that, with your high qualities, the great name of Portugal may continue.'

This telegram was published in all the papers. From what I know of this pilot who, although he was ten years older than

93

myself, was a colleague on my training course, I was not surprised that he seemed to believe our country was created in 1928 when Salazar took over as Finance Minister.

An invalid lieutenant in his sixties, Moreira Lopes, who was seriously wounded in the revolt on 7th February 1927, sent me a telegram as a counterblast to Baltazar's:

'As a combatant in the First World War, aide-de-camp to Marshal Gomes de Costa, wounded twice in battle, a prisoner-of-war of the Germans, captured on 9th April in France, a participant in the Portuguese revolts on 18th April, 19th June, 28th May and 7th February and, as a result of the latter, sent seriously wounded to the Military Hospital in the Estrela, decorated with the Torre e Espada, the Cruz de Guerra and many other medals, a companion, comrade and friend of Pilot Baltazar until the time of the Councils of War and our respective terms of imprisonment, I should like to offer my respects to General Humberto Delgado in whom are found the highest qualities necessary to increase the prestige of Portugal, and I pray God to grant him many years of life for the good of the Nation and the Portuguese people.'

Of course Salazar controls the censor and this telegram was never published. Yet the great democracies still seem to believe sometimes that Salazar is an absolute hero.

The fifth obstacle consisted of having no rights to the use of the wireless which stooped to any methods in order to broadcast propaganda in favour of the Government and prejudice the chances of the Opposition candidate. They even gave the time of my arrival in Oporto wrongly so as to muddle the people who were going to welcome me. Yet, despite this misleading information, I was greeted by an enormous mass of people, who, some said, numbered 200,000, but the photograph was never published in Portugal even during the 'free' electoral period.

The sixth obstacle concerned the actual voting-papers. Portugal is a poor country and a large number of the population either have a strong ambition to become civil servants or otherwise dependent upon the State. This results in an extraordinary political situation, for one cannot imagine the number of people who support the Opposition at heart, but fear reprisals. We were asked to take the greatest care to make it impossible to distinguish between the voting-papers for the two candidates, Admiral Tomás and myself, and so the paper had to be exactly the same colour, thickness and size. We ordered ours to be made from the same paper and with the same typography as the Government's candidate and, although we managed it, they were only delivered two or three days before the election. How were we supposed to get them to Madeira, the nearest island, or even to the northernmost parts of Portugal itself, where the daily paper is always a day late? A good number of the ballot-papers which we had printed in secret were rejected because they were some tenths of a millimetre different from the Government's. It seemed as if we had no chance.

The seventh method the Government employed to defraud the public was completely barefaced. In spite of all I have described they still feared they might lose and so they resorted to the very lowest tricks. P.I.D.E. installed spies near our headquarters to watch the cars taking the ballot-papers out for distribution in the suburbs and provinces and, as they drew away, they attacked them and seized the papers. One of their agents, well over six feet tall, even went so far as to enter our headquarters and try to steal packets of ballot-papers. Curiously enough, although there were many of my supporters all over the buildings, I was called from the 'President's Office' to get rid of him. He told me to take my hands off him, but only said it over his shoulder when he was half-way out of the door!

Their eighth tactic was to harass me. One night, the legionnaires came and painted a large 'S' in tar on my door, even though the police were supposed to be guarding the street. I telephoned them about it and also told them that I had been disturbed by someone ringing my door-bell during the night and, since they were not protecting me as they were other people, I should protect myself, if necessary using a revolver, if any of these cowardly tactics were repeated. This is the sort of low tricks that the Salazarist government uses against candidates for the Presidency; they try to intimidate them by harassing and humiliating them.

Once, when I was with my wife in a Lisbon cinema, the ordinary public alarm bell rang and I was told to go to the manager's office to take a phone call. (In normal circumstances it is unheard of to call a member of the audience to the telephone.) Apparently some of Salazar's cronies planned to set my house on fire and make an attempt on my life when I left the cinema.

Their ninth method was to terrorize the people so that they would be too frightened to cast their votes, thinking that if things were so bad before the elections, it would be dreadful on the actual day. When the people of Lisbon learnt how on my return from Oporto the Government had forced my car to follow the side roads and avoid the main streets and so prevent me from meeting the crowds waiting for me, they reacted very strongly, and took another road to my house where they held a demonstration to show their support. However, the police blocked the way into the Rossio, the main square, and then fired upon them. This also happened in Oporto.

Finally, we come to the tenth method of preventing my election which is by far the most original. On the morning of polling-day, 8th June 1958, the people were amazed at being told through official channels that members of the Opposition were not going to be allowed to supervise the voting. Consequently, as many people told me, as soon as the doors were closed after the voting, the supervisors switched the numbers and recorded my votes as being for the Government candidate. Everyone wondered why they bothered to have elections at all.

The Communist Party

At the beginning I was vigorously attacked by the Communists who, since they could not call me dishonest, stupid, ignorant or a bad administrator, said I was a Fascist. Yet is there any other army in the world which has asked *en masse* to resign because they were ruled by a dictatorship? Who can deny that a large number of people were completely taken aback when Salazar, as Minister of Finance, presented a balanced budget? I remember it well, although I was only twenty-three at the time. Can anyone dispute the fact that a large majority, including men from the 1910 Republic, supported or at least served the military dictatorship and even Dr Salazar? All this can be read in the contemporary newspapers in the National Library.

Although I was attacked by the Communists, who tried to create a public scene on one occasion at a banquet in Oporto, I was still accused of belonging to their party.

Dr Salazar's supporters tried to base their criticism upon the fact that I never ran the Communist Party down in my speeches, but my object was to stress that Communism in Portugal was essentially 'Fomismo'—an appeal to the hungry —as indeed it is. Nevertheless, I have always quite categorically stated that I do not support any totalitarian régime, whether red or white, acknowledging only the rights of individuals, not political groups, as my claim to be an independent candidate was meant to signify. It was because of this firm conviction that I appointed a monarchist, the university professor, Vieira de Almeida, as President of the Central Commission when the republicans in Oporto proposed him for the position.

Two more candidates

Cunha Leal, who has an extraordinary knowledge of mathematics and economics, as well as exceptional ability as a writer, was a highly respected figure, but he was not in good health when they persuaded him to stand for election. The other candidate was Dr Arlindo Vicente whom I will describe in detail later.

In an interview with the Radio Clube Portuguesa on 20th May, Cunha Leal was questioned upon his withdrawal from election and this was his answer:

'I am in favour of a modification of the present situation by means of an evolutionary and conciliatory process and nothing more. Since there are two Opposition candidates, I want to see them and their supporters mutually respect each other and I feel that it should be understood that at a certain stage of the campaign whichever of them has more support, the other should stand down in his favour. If in fact this does happen, then I believe that nothing will have been lost. In other words, "Man proposes and God disposes". The fact is that the momentous demonstrations in support of General Humberto Delgado, which make it clear that the country is behind him, have caused me to bring forward the date of my own withdrawal.

'I have therefore resolved to show my immediate, though worthless, support for General Humberto Delgado for whom our people have already shed their blood. I feel most strongly that the hour has come for the Opposition to unite around the man who has managed to make an impression upon the nation, which gives him an opportunity to bring about an improvement in our country. I hope that this view of the present situation will be forgiven by Dr Arlindo Vicente and his supporters who so kindly chose me as their candidate and who have been disappointed that the sudden decline in my health has rendered me incapable of any intense political activity.'

There were rumours that the Government were preparing once more to deceive the world by a Machiavellian ruse on the pretext of 'subversion of public order', their own description of the people's enthusiasm, which they had tried to damp with the bullets of the dictator's army. The Council of State was to announce that I was not suitable, and so I would be forced to stand down even though I was the most powerful of the candidates, as well as the most dangerous, as later events have proved, although the election fraud has kept me out of Belém Palace. At the same time the democracies would not be able to say that the Opposition had no candidate, for Dr A. Vicente would still be allowed to stand and, in fact, had been notified of this plan by the Minister of the Interior, Trigo de Negreiros. It was certainly a clever scheme.

On 29th May, Dr Vicente came to see me at Almada, on the opposite side of the Tagus from Lisbon, where I was holding a meeting; he was just returning home from one. He proposed that he would stand down if I agreed to certain conditions, which I shall give in detail later. He was a very pleasant person who, from complete obscurity as a lawyer, had suddenly appeared as one of the leading figures in the political field. I could never understand why he cast aspersions, slight as they were, upon me once or twice during the electoral campaign in which he had the support of the Communist Party, whilst I took care either not to mention him at all or if I did, to praise him. As I have said, I found him an agreeable person and I always stood up for him when, after he had retired from the elections, some people tried to deny him the respect due to an ex-candidate.

Thus two candidates remained, Admiral Tomás, supported by Dr Salazar, and myself, with the backing of the people.

The Foreign Press

In the next chapter I shall study the electoral campaign in detail, but here I should like to point out that the situation in Portugal was reported in papers all over the world, especially after the special correspondent of *As Folhas de São Paulo*, Sr Domingo de Lucca Junior, had been expelled from Portugal for bravely and forcefully pointing out the falseness of the régime at the most crucial moment of the campaign.

In one of his excellent articles, 'Five Days under the Heel of Salazar', he wrote: 'After an interview with the Portuguese Secretary of Information, Sr C. H. Moreira Batista, and his assistant, Sr Tavares de Almeida, I could guess that when my second telegram, which I sent on Election Day and left on the counter of Radio Marconi, found its way to their office, it would be seized, as the first one had been.

'. . . When I returned to my room about 8.15 p.m. on the same day (9th June) a P.I.D.E. official came to see me, but after carefully scrutinizing my passport, he left, only to come back a few minutes later and ask me to accompany him. When we were in the street, I asked if I might buy some cigarettes on the corner, but he would not let me, saying "We have some cigarettes in the P.I.D.E. offices".'

After hours of waiting at P.I.D.E. de Lucca saw a high official come in and then was given a long lecture which, as he wrote, 'repeated what the Secretary of Information had already told me, namely that General Humberto Delgado was not completely sane.' Certainly, according to the materialist

Salazar doctrine, one would have to be insane to give up the comforts of a generalship for the equivalent of a lieutenant's pay in a civilian job, when in exile in Brazil.

The journalist did not agree and so he described the interview he had had with me two days before on the eve of the elections:

' "After the 9th I don't know what will happen to me, for there has never been a general on the active list who has opposed the Government, but I am ready for anything." These were the final words that General Humberto Delgado said to us on the 7th, the eve of the elections, at his home in Lisbon. He was tired. He is of medium height, with a lively and alert mind. Despite signs of the turbulent campaign he has just been through, he replied unhesitatingly and objectively to all our questions.'

What a difference from the other opinions!

PART THREE

CHAPTER X

My electoral campaign

JOURNALISTS throughout the world reported that something new was happening in Portugal. Firstly, if age is of any consequence, the Opposition had the youngest of the three candidates who had ever tried to compete with those chosen by the dictator: Norton de Matos had been eighty-one in 1949, Quintão Meireles seventy-one in 1951, but in May 1958 I was only fifty-two.

Secondly, if one's profession counts, the first candidate was an officer in the Army, the second in the Navy and I was in the Air Force.

Thirdly, the first two candidates were retired and not even on the reserve, whilst I was an officer on the active list with another dozen years to go before I reached retirement age.

Finally, and most important, I was very much an extrovert, seasoned by many years of service abroad, where I had lived in the great democratic countries and worked under parliamentary systems on international committees.

I should add that this was the first time in thirty-two years of dictatorship that the Opposition candidate had actually stood for election and competed with the Government right through until polling-day, for the other two had withdrawn on the eve of the elections. Yet Norton de Matos had worked in close contact with the people, as the meeting in Oporto had proved, while Meireles had conducted his campaign chiefly by communiqués. When I suddenly appeared in the lists, full of exuberance and high spirits, the Salazarists reproachfully nicknamed me the 'cow-boy'.

The campaign opened with a flourish on 10th May in the Chave de Ouro Café in Lisbon. Dozens of journalists were present and in the places of honour were many republicans of the old school, such as Antonio Sérgio, Jaime Cortesão, Azevedo Gomes and Aquilino Ribeiro, the novelist. On my right sat my General Secretary, Artur Andrade. Of course no officers on the active list were present, as could only be expected when one considers how many were openly involved in the campaign of my opponent, Adm. Américo Tomás, but there were two high-ranking Air Force reserve officers, Ribeiro da Fonseca and António Maia, also my political agent, Dr Sebastião Ribeiro, the lawyer, and many women, including my wife. To her I offer my deepest gratitude, for she overcame her distaste for politics in order to accompany me in this historic campaign, thus setting an example to the women of Portugal to whom I have dedicated a few words of praise in my 'Proclamation to the Portuguese People'.

The banners, the enthusiasm, the hope that we might win in spite of all the pre-election obstacles I have described, in short, everything combined to arouse an atmosphere *sui generis*. Yet, just one insulting word, and all civilized courtesy would have vanished in a flash, like a barrel of gunpowder when the lighted fuse reaches it. In fact this almost happened when the correspondent of Franco's *ABC* decided to heckle us and, irritated by the shouting of our supporters, asked whether we were having a party meeting or a press conference. However, I managed to quieten him and keep control of myself.

The day before, we had discussed what I ought to reply if as was bound to happen some journalist should ask what I would do with the Prime Minister, Dr Salazar, if we won the election. Some, still believing that serious elections might be allowed, had suggested that I soften my words, for we might win another 100 or 1,000 votes that way. Poor ingenuous creatures! Naturally, Salazar had his own uniformed puppet of a candidate and would announce the election results in any figures he thought fit.

Inevitably the question came up but I had my reply ready: '*Obviously, I should dismiss him.*'

There was an overwhelming outburst of enthusiasm: for years the people had secretly harboured that thought, but through justifiable fear or extraordinary astuteness, it had never been spoken aloud. Now it seemed as if a volcano had erupted.

The agencies telegraphed my words to the furthermost parts of the world and I was told by a member of the Brazilian Federal Parliament, Saul Diniz, member for Minas Gerais, that my photograph had even found its way into the newspaper of Communist China.

'Long live the fearless General' became the slogan. Such are the peculiarities of mass psychology that such a simple phrase became the basis for the whole campaign.

I shall show briefly now how clownish, puerile and ridiculous Salazar's forces were, for this phrase was taken as a direct affront to him and gave rise to tactics which he called a 'campaign of redress', and which would have been more fitting in a circus. The dictator was flooded with telegrams which, so it was said, were ordered by Santos Costa, the Defence Minister and by the National Union. Telegrams which actually came from the High Commands of the Army were sent in the name of their subordinates and thus the upper ranks showed that they considered the main body of officers as nothing more than a flock of sheep, even though they too had the right to vote in an election for the President of the Republic. One telegram read: 'Allow me to assure Your Excellency how strongly I objected to the disgracefully rude declaration which Sr General Humberto Delgado made in the newspapers that if he were elected he would dismiss Your Excellency.'

This means that anyone running for the Presidency might become Head of State but could not dismiss the Prime Minister, even though the latter had already been in office for thirty years. We shall see about that!

On 14th May I left for Oporto and when I remember my arrival there, pictures flash through my mind like scenes from a film—the faces of the veterans of our campaign. I should like to quote João Alvez das Neves, reporting for the *Estado de São Paulo*: 'Certain papers in the capital had hinted, but only between the lines, that 200,000 people had jubilantly welcomed General Humberto Delgado in Oporto. The Oporto morning paper, *O Primeiro de Janeiro*, which carried a detailed account of his arrival, was sold out almost as soon as it was on the streets in Lisbon.

'After that came silence. The violence with which the speakers of the National Union delivered their speeches in Vila Nova de Gaia on the night after Humberto Delgado's arrival in the northern capital seemed to show that the members of the "Establishment" were afraid and apprehensive of the demonstration by such a large proportion of the population of the "Invincible City". There was talk of collisions between the police and the people, of shooting and casualties.'

I was passed from shoulder to shoulder and eventually reached the covered car which was to take me to Carlos Alberto Square, the site of our headquarters. There were shouts, tears, and a great outburst of enthusiasm; this was indeed like the Portugal of the earliest days, seeking her independence from Spain or, as in the reign of D. Pedro IV, struggling for liberty.

As soon as we arrived, Dr Eduardo Santos Silva, a former minister of the Republic, Colonel Helder Ribeiro, another former Minister, and Artur Mirandela, a very popular figure, spoke to the people.

That night we held a meeting in the Coliseum of Oporto where a mass of people squeezed and pushed so hard to find a way in that they even burst the doors open. There were four speeches by Carlos Cal Brandão, one of the most brutally persecuted victims of the P.I.D.E., Rolão Preto, a monarchist with some socialist views, Major David Neto of the reserves, who had been a supporter of Salazar, and the young Dr João Araujo Correia of the 'third force'.

As soon as Correia had finished, the police, worried because of the enthusiasm, tried to turn all those who were standing out of the room. However, there were as many people standing as there were seated and so Artur Andrade put forward a conciliatory proposal that we would omit two of the speakers, Professor Vieira de Almeida and Dr Vasco de Gama Fernandez.

The atmosphere was tense and explosive when I got up to speak and it was difficult to obtain silence. In a tribute to Arlindo Vicente, who was still at the speakers' table, I began by quoting one of his sayings, referring to Salazar and his Minister, Santos Costa: 'The country cannot belong to two men alone.' I professed to be confident of victory in the elections, in spite of everything, for what else could I say?

The Church

I referred to the words of Pope Pius VII: 'There are certain personal rights and liberties, either of the individual or of the family, which the State must always protect and cannot violate or sacrifice to any so-called law of the general well-being.' D. António, Bishop of Oporto, who later was to write the famous letter opposing Salazar, was very fond of these words, while the dictator must have loathed them. I pointed out the apparent paradox that although the population of the patriarchate had risen by 33% between 1930 and 1957, the number of Portuguese priests had only increased by 7%. 'The loss of liberty affects everything, even our faith.'

The economy

In the chapter on the Portuguese economy I have explained that in spite of the stability of the escudo our country had the lowest standard of living in Europe. In my speech I gave the statistics proving this and dealt with the problems of housing, national assistance, disability and old age, which have always been neglected in Portugal. Then, to make sure that everyone understood I added: 'Germany, Belgium, France, Holland, and Norway have all been recently overrun and, so Salazar's supporters proudly tell us, their currency is less stable. But at least the people of those countries do have some money in their pockets. The escudo is stable all right but who has any escudos?

'We sent ships to India, but our fleet is too small. Yet Norway didn't go there, nor did Greece, although they have the third and fourth largest fleets in the world. Yes, gentlemen, we are lagging behind, in spite of the cork and the wolfram, the sardines, the Port and the brandy that we sold to both sides during the war. Where did all that money go? All into the pockets of no more than a hundred families.'

Politics

I explained the Opposition's basic programme and clearly stated: 'To those poor ignorant souls who demand a detailed programme, I would simply like to say that I have no wish to be a dictator; it is up to the nation to explain, through the legitimate channels, what they want. I am only one instrument, not the whole orchestra.

'As for those who ask for a complete explanation of how we shall deal with Communism, I shall simply tell them to read my manifesto and to remember that in Scandinavia, for example, where a truly free democracy exists, there are hardly any Communists even though it is so close to Russia. Why? Because there is social justice. However, everyone knows that the Communists have built up a campaign against me and are still doing so.'

Aiming my words at Dr Salazar and his acolytes, I bitterly cried: 'It's time for them to go. We are sick of them. Out with them! Throw them out!'

This rousing, fiery style elated the masses and stunned the Salazarists and there was one sentence in particular from an interview I had with the Lisbon newspaper *A República*, published on 10th May, which especially annoyed them. Referring scathingly to Portuguese youth, I said that Salazar brands them at the age of ten with an 'S' on the belt-buckles of their uniforms, just as a farmer brands his cattle on their haunches to show who owns them.

On the 10th May, my 52nd birthday, I paid a friendly call on Father Américo's Catholic Social Centre, where orphan boys are looked after extremely well and, for this, I was immediately accused by the Salazarists of being a hypocritical demagogue for pretending so late in the day to be concerned about the misfortune of these children. Yet when I arrived at Father Américo's institution one of the boys came up to me with a smile and told me that they had discovered that I was one of the oldest subscribers to their paper, *O Gaiato*, which the children publish to help the Institution and, more-

over, according to their list I was still only a lieutenant-
colonel.

Now things began to move at a hectic pace. On the 16th
I visited Póvoa and here the National Republican Guard
first showed their complete servility to Salazar, disgracing
their uniforms, for even my old comrades in the Army who
were serving in that company held up the procession of cars
accompanying me and forced me to enter the town alone. I
have many debts to settle one day. . . .

Shooting in Lisbon

The same day I went on to Lisbon and at this point I shall
again let the reporter, João Alves das Neves, describe this
visit, by quoting from his article, 'I was in Lisbon'.

'Early on that unforgettable Friday afternoon the word
flashed through the streets, cafés and offices that General
Humberto was arriving back from Oporto at 6.30. And
suddenly everyone started to talk, as if they were tired of
their usual silence which they had kept for so many years.

' "Are you going to wait for Delgado?" they asked and
everyone answered "Yes".

'The black line of people grew at an astounding rate and,
like a trail of lighted gunpowder, the news spread to Rua
Augusts that General Delgado had had to come by a different
route.

'Suddenly along the street the horses of the National
Republican Guard appeared and the soldiers, as if possessed,
were slashing wildly to left and right with their swords. The
police did the same, but the crowd was not frightened and
did not scatter, for they were simply dumbfounded.

'But after a few moments of complete astonishment, the city
at last woke from its stupor and the first shouts arose of "Long
live liberty! Down with Fascism! Long live democracy!"
The fury of the police and the National Republican Guard
increased until finally the troops fired into the crowd. Then,
like the howl of an animal which, although wounded and
bloody, is not yet defeated, the cry arose: "Murderers!
Murderers!" Many had been taken by surprise and had been

wounded in the shooting and now they lay, unable to get up, while others rushed into the adjoining streets. Some had managed to pull up paving-stones to throw at their attackers. Cars and lapels sported paper emblems bearing the portrait of General Delgado.

'The crowd did not run away, but retreated down one street only to advance along another. Thousands of young men in this unequal battle shouted the names of Delgado, Liberty and Democracy, and tried to get to the party head-quarters in the Avenida da Liberdade in the hope of seeing General Humberto Delgado.'

That night I received a phone call telling me that P.I.D.E. were attacking our headquarters and, although I was exhausted by all the dashing around, which seemed more like a Western film than a political campaign, I immediately took the lift downstairs, but the road was blocked by troops with machine-guns and when I tried to get out three members of P.I.D.E. stood in my way. I caught hold of one of them by the neck, hoping to strangle him, but his friends dragged him away.

On the 18th we held a meeting in the Camões School in Lisbon, since the Government had forbidden us to hold one in the open, and here we encountered the same feverish atmosphere which the events of the 16th had only served to increase. After the meeting, the unarmed civilians, who wanted nothing more than to see the Opposition's candidate, were again fired upon and attacked with swords.

Support

As a compensation for the decision of the Social Democratic Directorate, which I have described earlier, that they would 'actively abstain' in the electoral campaign, many unofficial groups as well as many individuals of all classes were giving us their support, for they realized that normal party politics no longer existed. One anonymous lady used actually to send me a rose at our headquarters every day.

Some officers secretly gave us their moral support, but the majority either unhesitatingly obeyed their orders brutally to suppress the people, even though these were responsible for their wages, or else sunk into a convenient apathy which Santana Mota, a reporter for the *Estado de São Paulo*, was to condemn so violently.

The *New York Times*, contemptuous of the whole wretched business, said: 'Gen. Humberto Delgado, fifty-two years old, the most senior general in the Air Force, has retained the reputation of bravery which has been his since he became one of the first pilots in the country in 1926. What he has done is to awaken Portugal, and this is the greatest thing that has happened there in thirty years.'

My return to Oporto

When I set out on the 21st, P.I.D.E., who were by now thoroughly frightened, sent the terrifying Inspector Porto Duarte to Lisbon airport, when I was about to board the plane, in order to advise me not to stay at the Infante Sagres Hotel in Oporto, but at another one in the suburbs such as the Matozinhos which was near the airport, for he warned me that if I did not do so, the police would not hold themselves responsible for my safety. I replied that I would go to the Infante Sagres and manage without their protection.

Although Oporto looked as if it were in a state of war with so many troops and police in the streets, some motor-cycles and cars managed to break through the police cordons and, by driving on the pavements, accompany me to the city centre. This resulted in more shooting and fighting with swords and rifle-butts, but by now this had become commonplace.

The marathon begins

On the 22nd I visited Chaves, Amarante, where I was showered with so many petals that we nearly suffocated, Vila Real, Murça, Mirandela, Pinhais and Bragança. (On the journey between these last two towns I was protected with a pistol in case the P.I.D.E. car should pull over too close, for it was a mountain road along steep precipices and a slight push could pitch me over the edge.)

On the 23rd I went to Macedo de Cavaleiros, Lamego, Régua and Vizeu, where youngsters from the Portuguese

Youth Movement, with hatred in their eyes, defied my remarks about their 'S' buckles by parading in their uniforms.

On the 24th I entered Lisbon by way of Vila Franca de Xira and one scene remains indelibly fixed in my mind. The P.I.D.E. car cut through my procession and kept on my tail, so to provoke them I stopped, turned round and then turned back again, just like a rabbit and a terrier. How I would have liked to send half a dozen bullets into their radiator. How much I had to endure!

On 26th May a great argument arose as to whether I should go to Braga, where Santos Costa was stationed with thousands of men all ready and waiting for me, for he knew that the roads would be closed to me, so that when the legionnaires attacked me at the entrance to the city I should have none of my supporters to help me against this band of ruffians. People telephoned me from all sides begging me to cancel the journey, but I insisted on going and accepting the challenge, even though my agent in Braga himself tried to prevent me. On the 27th Braga was like a city in mourning; all the doors and windows were closed and there was not a soul to be seen except the usual coach-loads of children from the orphanages, who are always used on such occasions. Santos Costa was shouting out his speech saying that the nation belonged to him and his supporters and, as for us, we were nothing more than a horde of unpatriotic rebels.

On the 28th I was in Almada, across the Tagus from Lisbon. Arlindo Vicente proposed that he should stand down on certain conditions which I willingly accepted, since they were no different from those I had already stated in my proclamation. The only new proviso was that I should make a formal declaration that unless some major problem prevented it the next general elections would be held within a year. (The date had not been fixed before but it was as well to do it now. . . .)

I should like to mention at this point that the Government had prepared an astute plan whereby they would call a Council of State and pronounce me unfit for candidature on the grounds that I was responsible for causing the firing upon the crowd. Then they were going to propose my colleague, Arlindo Vicente, as candidate, knowing that he was far less popular than I and less likely to win the election, thus making the Government's return inevitable. The Minister himself, Trigo de Negreiros, had told Vicente this in an interview with him. However, if the Government eliminated me now that Vicente had stood down, there would be no opposition in the elections and the dictator could hardly deceive the great democracies as easily as that. We went to my home and signed the agreement and once Vicente had withdrawn from the elections, the Communist Party changed its attitude towards me.

On the 30th I visited Covilhã and Guarda, where I received an overwhelming reception from the workers, but learnt that P.I.D.E. had raided my Lisbon headquarters. On the 31st I was in Gouveia, Covilhã and Coimbra, where Dr Rodrigo de Abreu, a great friend of mine at that time, who had accompanied me on my travels throughout the country, brought me a message that P.I.D.E. wanted to talk to me. I refused to meet them personally, saying that I did not talk to dogs. Then de Abreu informed me that P.I.D.E. said I could not go back to Braga the next day, but I replied: 'Tell them that unless I receive a written order from the Government I shall leave at 9 tomorrow morning even if I have to use force.' Strangely enough this was arranged in a very short time, for I was given a written order from the Commander of the Military Region, General Souza Gomes, forbidding me to return to Braga.

In Coimbra I received the terrible news that all those who were to carry out the revolt on 2nd June had withdrawn.

On 1st June I had to enter Lisbon alone, thanks to the manoeuvring of the police and the Army.

The south of the Tagus remains to be won

On the 3rd I travelled through Évora, Alcáçovas, Aljustrel and Faro and orders to the police were so strict that they allowed only my car to pass through their road-blocks, for in this way they hoped to separate me from the people. P.I.D.E.'s agents, in dark glasses and with pale, scowling faces, were all over the town and the hotel and it cost me a tremendous effort not to strangle any of them.

On the 4th I visited the fishing towns of Algoz, Silves, Portimão and Vila Real de Santo António, where the hungry crowds held up their children, half-starved and emaciated through lack of vitamins, bread and even milk, as if I could infuse life into them like a saint. I saw the widow of Heremias, who had been my batman, dressed in mourning and hollow-cheeked through hunger and lack of money. I set out for the country district of Beja where starvation was widespread, but the crowd was so closely packed around my car that we could not go on. So I got out and was carried shoulder-high for nearly a mile.

My return and the end of the campaign

On the 5th I learnt that Artur Andrade and the members of the Committees of Chaves, Braga and Guimarães had been arrested by P.I.D.E., who had used all possible methods to intimidate my supporters and persuade them not to take part in the election. I set out for Lisbon, for the campaign was over. Through Dr Rodrigo de Abreu P.I.D.E. ordered me not to leave the house without permission but I refused, and on the 6th the police actually began to attack the cars which were distributing the ballot-forms. I learnt that while I was away, Da Maria Pia de Saxe-Coburg, the daughter of King Carlos I and a modern monarchist with liberal ideas, had paid me a courtesy call in order to show her support for my campaign.

On the 8th, the day of the elections, the Government published their famous bulletin forbidding the Opposition to inspect the voting procedure. Need I say more about this shameless trickery and the curtailment of the people's rights?

The *New York Times* wrote on the 10th: 'General Delgado naturally lost by a large majority of votes to the candidate chosen by António de Oliveira Salazar, dictator and Prime Minister. The name of the victor happens to be Rear-Admiral Américo Tomás, but this is of no importance whatsoever. He will have no power and Dr Salazar could just as well have chosen the first traffic policeman he came across.'

On the 14th Domingos de Lucca published an article in the *Folha da Manhã* entitled: 'The Presidential elections on the 8th were a mere farce.' Various other papers, such as the

New Statesman in London, *L'Intransigeant, Libération* and *L'Express* in Paris, all expressed similar views.

Immediately after the elections the Minister of Defence automatically dismissed me from my post as Director-General of Civil Aviation and also from my position in the Ministry of Communications. Then, with his usual audacity, Dr Salazar said in a speech shortly afterwards that the Opposition had lost the elections in spite of their underhand tricks! Since it would have seemed odd if he announced that I had received no votes at all, he decided to grant me 236,528 against the 758,998 of Adm. Américo Tomás, but everyone said that it should have been the other way around.

I cannot understand how that man can still sleep at night.

CHAPTER XI

My election protest

THE reader will probably be wondering why, as a General, I did not seek the support of the President of the Republic who was also a General of the Armed Forces. In fact I wrote several letters to him protesting strongly about the suppression of my articles and speeches during the so-called thirty days freedom the Government allows the Opposition, the forbiddance of free access to the electoral rolls, and the despicable behaviour of the police. I urged him to use his constitutional rights to dismiss the Government so that free, honest elections could be held. I received no reply.

It was to the President of the Republic that I sent the petition in protest against the elections, for the sake of history and also as a means of encouraging, provoking and creating an atmosphere suitable for eventual beneficial action. I shall not explain now why I sent it to the President and not to the courts, but I should like to state that there is no law under which the election fraud could be punished—in fact there is no law in the true sense of the word at all in Portugal. Law is based upon the supposition that at least in theory the State defends the rights of the people, but when the law, to mention only one factor, is created by someone who is determined to remain in power until death forces him to relinquish it, then there is no way of appeal other than by force of arms or direct application to the Head of State, provided that he has any real authority. Neither Carmona nor Lopes were actually the Head of State but merely military figure-heads.

The protest

This is dated 21st June 1958, thirteen days after the election, and will be put into the national archives as evidence of the shameless methods of the Salazarists. It gives a detailed, factual account of events which I have described in an earlier chapter. Here are some extracts:

'Sr President of the Republic

'Excellency:

Falsification of the Election Results

'The presidential elections in which I ran as independent candidate were carried out in a manner which completely misrepresented the will of the nation, which the enormous popular demonstrations during my electoral campaign made blatantly obvious. Your Excellency has undoubtedly been told of these, for even the humblest Portuguese knows about them although the Government in its fright took the unthinkable step of prohibiting publication of the photographs showing my triumphant arrival in Oporto, at which, according to a French observer, more than 200,000 people were present.

'For example:

'*a*) The electoral roll was at the same time incomplete and extensible.

'The mainland of Portugal has approximately nine million inhabitants so that, making due allowance for those without the franchise especially the women, the numbers of electors should still be around two to two and a half million. Yet, although there were only a few abstentions, the number of votes recorded at the polling-stations, according to the Government, was minimal; being only 1,001,138. (In Lisbon, with approximately 900,000 inhabitants, only 105,978 voted and in Oporto, with 400,000, 27,167 voted.)

'The complete list of frauds would be endless but, as examples, I shall mention the following:

'—In Viseu 138 nuns were put on the electoral roll

although they do not seem to fulfil the conditions required for women to vote.

'—In S. Vicente, Cape Verde Islands, the franchise was granted to priests and sacristans who had arrived from the capital only a few days before the election, whilst many of the voters who had been included on the roll for the last election of deputies were excluded from the presidential one.

'—In Luanda some 40% of the electors were not enrolled.

'—In Palmela the lists, as seen surreptitiously, carried three hundred names, but on election day six hundred were registered.

'—In Aveiro innumerable electors were not allowed to vote on the pretext that they were not on the roll, although they had been a few weeks before when a partial copy was made by the Opposition.

> '*b*) The Opposition is forbidden to copy the electoral roll or is only allowed to do so under impossible conditions. Many other difficulties, some of which were insurmountable, were put in their way.
> 'The Opposition, which is permanently forbidden any organization at all, was only allowed something approaching it during the thirty short days before the elections.'

At this point I mentioned the censorship, the prohibition of open-air meetings, the impossibility of using the wireless, the ban on posters, processions and the copying of the electoral rolls and the obligation to print our own ballot-papers.

I concluded:

> 'These facts are common knowledge and thus there is no need for Your Excellency to verify them for you must be aware of them already.
> '... Excellency, was this an election or a farce, as the newspapers called it in Portuguese (in Brazil, of course), English, French and Spanish—in fact from all over the world.

'Excellency, is this an independent, civilized nation or an uncivilized land under foreign occupation, kept under control by force of arms and police, who outrageously insult the intelligence and also the constitutional rights of the people?

'*c*) It is made difficult for the Opposition and easy for the National Union to distribute the ballot-papers which are essential in order to vote.

'Not only was the Opposition candidate allowed only seventy-two hours to distribute his ballot-papers to electors over a wide area, but even more difficulties were put in his way.'

In this paragraph I mentioned the arrests and the general atmosphere of terror and added:

'We possess a telegram from the district commission which gives adequate proof that illegal methods were used to hinder the delivery of ballot-papers to Funchal because they were made subject to an import tax.'

I continued with full details of this example of widespread political banditry:

'The ballot-papers arrived in Funchal in four packages, which were sealed and stamped by the Lisbon Post Office, on the *S. Miguel* at approximately 8 o'clock on the 7th, and we asked permission from the Customs to unload them. They were sent to the Customs House and handed over to the postal authorities at about 11 o'clock, but they refused to accept them and gave no explanation. Consequently the papers were sent back to the Customs who only agreed to clear them as merchandise subject to import tax, which we paid. Therefore in spite of all our efforts we only gained possession of the parcels, whose contents were quite obvious, at about 3.0 p.m. on the eve of the elections and thus suffered an irreparable setback, for they could be prepared and partially distributed only in the district of Funchal.'

This seems quite incredible. I continued:

'According to the report of our committee in Bissau, Government ballot-papers were distributed to the 107 soldiers stationed there, but permission was refused for the Opposition to do the same.

'*d*) The Opposition candidate is forbidden to use personal propaganda.

'The propaganda programme for the Opposition inevitably suffered not only from the arbitrary and illegal restrictions which the Government and its supporters imposed upon it, but also from the fact that it could only be organized at short notice on a temporary basis. Therefore it was absolutely essential for the candidate to visit as many parts of the country as possible in order to make up for the small amount of propaganda which the sponsoring committee was able to arrange. However, although I was a general on active service, who had been highly praised by both the Portuguese and foreign governments, I was followed all over the country by cars driven by P.I.D.E. agents who prevented me from making contact with the people and forced me to alter my planned route and take by-roads and deserted lanes.

'. . . Obviously P.I.D.E. did not accompany me in order to protect me from any attempt on my life, as was proved by my experience in Oporto and other towns, notably Gouveia, Covilhã and Beja, where I was surrounded by frantic crowds trying to embrace me.

'Moreover, as I warned my family, in the event of an attempt upon my life they should not conduct an inquiry along the lines suggested by P.I.D.E., namely against the Communist Party who had far more suitable targets, but rather against P.I.D.E. themselves or their secret agents. I based this advice upon the numerous incidents of foul play and high-handedness to which I was subjected without the least provocation.'

I then described the following occurrences, uncertain

whether they should be called infamous or merely grotesque:

'*e*) Violence and irregularities occurred on the vast majority of the polling-stations.

'Considering the difficulties which the Opposition had to surmount in order to distribute their ballot-papers, it was quite unnecessary for the National Union to commit irregularities in the actual polling-stations to ensure winning the election. Yet, as an extra precaution, the supporters of the régime decided to give the Opposition no chance whatsoever and so those few ballot-papers which did manage to reach the electors were to a large extent seized, annulled, torn up or destroyed while the voters were actually depositing them in the ballot-box. Moreover, the National Union illegally and even forcibly withdrew Opposition members from the electoral roll and replaced them with their own supporters.

'Here are a few examples:

'—In S. Vicente, Cape Verde Islands, Salazarists broke the law by distributing their ballot-papers in the actual polling-station and even took the Opposition papers away from the electors who had brought them and replaced them with their own. The electors were so frightened by the arrests and warnings during the preceding days that they accepted the substitution without any resistance.

'—In Mujãe (Viana do Castelo) the returning officer opened the papers as he received them and tore up all those which were not for the Government candidate.

'—On several occasions people voted on behalf of absent or indisposed members of their family; protests made against the irregularities of the elections were ignored and the ballot-boxes, when full, were emptied in another room and returned to be refilled.

'—In S. Jacinto, where the voters consisted of airmen from the nearby base and a large number of the workers in the naval shipyards, it was calculated that the Opposition would have a large majority. Therefore the elector appointed as witness to the proceedings was sent away and not allowed to be present when the votes were counted. Here is a typical telegram of protest sent to the Minister of the Interior: "In the name of General Delgado's Opposition in the district of Viana in the municipality of Cerveira, I wish to inform Your Excellency that a large number of ballot-papers were rejected on the excuse that their size was not correct. The papers of the Opposition were checked by an official measure and I can verify that those of Admiral Américo Tomás were larger than the legal size. In the parish of Lanhelas in the municipality of Caminha, the Admiral received only fifty-five votes whilst the General gained 126, but after the count this was reduced to 17 on the same excuse that the size of the ballot-papers was not correct. On behalf of my committee and in the name of justice, I present Your Excellency with my most heart-felt protest."

'But there were many other injustices:

'—In Eixo (Aveiro) the doctor who acted as returning officer inspected the papers before they were placed in the ballot-box and, if they were for the Opposition, he made the voter take a National Union paper and put it in the box instead.

'—In Rio Tinto (Oporto) where the electorate were amazed to learn that 452 votes had been attributed to the National Union and only 150 to the Opposition, when it was obvious that the electors had voted en masse for the Opposition candidate, the returning officer ordered the papers to be burnt in the actual building where the polling had taken place.

'—In Valbom (Gondomar) when the voting was over, the returning officer emptied the box on to a patch of floor surrounded by desks and after the officials had picked them up there were found to be 430, whereas only 246 had been deposited in the box.

'f) Apart from all these irregularities, in almost all the polling-stations members of the Opposition were forbidden to witness the voting.

'If there had been inspectors at the polling-stations, many of these irregularities would have been impossible and official protests would have been made against those that were committed, but the Minister of the Interior would not allow my agents to be present. As things turned out, the Opposition was only able to witness a minute part of the illegal practices, but the following alone is sufficient to annul the votes which the National Union claimed for their candidate:

'—In Luanda, where inspectors were allowed, nearly 40% of the electorate voted, whereas in former elections, when the Opposition had not acted as witness, the Government had claimed that between 80% and 99% had voted.

'g) Apart from the above, coercive action was imposed upon the electors at the actual voting-boxes.

'The Salazarists did not hesitate to intervene at the very last moment before the papers were placed in the box and subject the electors to coercion by surrounding the table on which the ballot-box stood with P.I.D.E. agents and legionnaires.

'Here are some examples:

'—In Santa Maria (Setúbal) a P.I.D.E. agent came up to the Opposition inspectors and, claiming they were Communist elements, ordered them to leave the polling-station and threatened to arrest them if they did not obey.

'—In Cacia the workers in the Portuguese Cellulose Company, who had shown their support of the Opposition candidate during the election campaign, were ordered to work on election day, a Sunday, and were thus prevented from voting.

'—In Vista Alegre, where many of the voters were factory workers, the supervision was carried out by trusted employees of the directors who were themselves present during the voting. The day before, these directors had ordered the papers for the National Union candidate to be enclosed in sealed envelopes which were to be opened only just before the voting. Although this order was later revoked, many of the workers still came to the polling-station with their sealed envelopes.

'*h*) The nauseating absurdities of the election, caused by fraud and the fact that the Opposition is only allowed to exist for thirty days once every seven years.

'This section, Excellency, is intended to prove that intelligence, perception and honesty must prevent one from accepting the results of the ridiculous election of 8th June. Thus, as a basic test of the Government's honesty, I should like to draw your attention to the fact that the number of votes recorded is equal to the number of potential electors, signifying that they claimed the whole of the electorate had voted, rather than an individual count being made. Yet I must point out that in Angola we won in Luanda, Lobito, Benguela and Sá de Bandeira, and in Mozambique, in Beira, Manica, Sofala, Tete, Quelimane, Inhambane and Mozambique City.

'On the other hand we lost in Lisbon, in spite of the demonstration which, although I was not allowed to take part in it, was quashed by the public authorities who fired upon and attacked those involved because the Government was afraid of the enormous crowds who wanted to welcome me. Similarly, the Government said that I lost in Oporto, of all places, the traditional bulwark of liberty, where my candidature took shape and where, according to some observers, 200,000 people waited for me when I first visited the city to open the electoral campaign. Who could honestly believe this?

'The dishonesty is self-apparent for, while the Government claimed that I was defeated here, they could not deny that I won in Vila Nova de Gaia, a small town separated from Oporto by just one small bridge. I state once more that whenever even the minimum lawful inspection was permitted it immediately became obvious that the nation wanted to free itself from the chains of the dictatorship.

'Even more flagrant is the manner in which the Government claimed that from the 400,000 or so inhabitants of Oporto I gained only 8,865 votes, whilst in the small town of Vila Nova de Gaia, with about a tenth of Oporto's population, they recorded 7,768 in my favour, almost as many as in the city.

'—The figures for the Azores show: in Nordeste 1,235 for the Government and none for me; in Povoaçáo 1,703 and 2; in Pico 739 and nil; in Horta 4,895 and nil.

'—In Cape Verde Islands 13,191 and 214, or, in other words, 97·6% for Sr Américo Tomás. These figures remind one of the Communist elections on the other side of the Iron Curtain.

'—In S. Tomé and Príncipe 5,620 or 100% for Tomás.

'—In the State of India (note the grandiose title for Goa!) 16,773 and 765 respectively, or 95% for Tomás.

'Excellency, is there anyone in the country, including Admiral Américo Tomás himself, who can honestly believe that these figures represent the real desires of the nation although, admittedly, a few are quite correct, for my voting-papers were never allowed to reach certain distant parts of Portuguese territory?'

In the *Estado de São Paulo*, Santana Mota described the situation like this:

'Last Sunday the Portuguese curtain, which for thirty days has been lifted in order to give a divided and troubled world the edifying example of "peaceable and democratic" elections, fell once more. The result is obvious, for the winner was, inevitably, the official candidate but, although the Opposition claims that the election was a fraud, the Government denies it. Yet, taking into account the means at the disposal of the two parties, it is not difficult to judge who is right. But, for the sake of argument, let us say that the Government's assertions are correct and that the genuine voting showed that in Lisbon 73,896 voted for the Admiral and 24,572 for the General, in Coimbra 7,111 and 4,228 respectively and in Oporto 18,302 and 8,865. These figures do not exactly signify what the Government would like us to believe, for the votes attributed to General Delgado, few as they are, were all placed by electors who were confidently considered as Government supporters because, of course, no one else has the honour of appearing on the electoral rolls. But can anyone possibly imagine that Lisbon, with more than a million inhabitants, has only 100,000 citizens qualified to vote?'

To continue:

'Coercion on the part of the Government

'During my campaign around the country, difficulties were constantly being put in my path even to the extent of being forbidden to go to Braga on 1st and 2nd June, which were the only dates possible for me, and also I was not allowed to hold a meeting in Beja, in spite of the wild enthusiasm of the population. Meanwhile, however, the ministers, under-secretaries and members of the National union, who were making capital out of the state of terror in which the country constantly lives, found every facility at their disposal.

'The assessment of the elections and Government by the foreign press

'... In thirty days of freedom the mask was snatched from the face of the Government. There were some newspapers whose insistence caused them to be suspected of being subsidized; and others which had no correspondent here. Apart from these, Your Excellency must be aware of the wave of attack that assailed the Portuguese Government, and the farce of the election.

'To cite a few examples:

'—In the United States: *The New York Times, Washington Post, Daily Herald, Star* and *Time*

'—In Brazil: *Correio da Manhã, Diário de Notícias, Estado de São Paulo*

'—In France: *Figaro, Le Monde, Paris Presse-L'Intransigeant, L'Express, France Observateur*

'—In England: *The Times*, *Manchester Guardian*, *News Chronicle*, *Daily Herald*, *Observer*, *New Statesman*, *Reynolds' News*

'—In Switzerland: *Tribune de Lausanne*, *Tribune de Genève*

'The Government lost a serious amount of prestige by this support of the National Independent candidate, support which was freely given, for I was too poor to be able to buy it, being hard-pressed even to give modest sums to the families of the many political prisoners whom the Government had arrested during the electoral campaign.

'Conclusions

'These facts, combined with many others which any serious investigator could verify, lead to several obvious conclusions

'... Despite the shameless misrepresentation of the election results, the Government was forced to declare that the independent candidate obtained 23·5% of the votes. No one could doubt that I was the more popular candidate, if to this percentage were added all the votes falsely entered in favour of the Government candidate, those in favour of myself which were unlawfully annulled and those not allowed to be registered because the ballot-papers did not reach various places in time or because coercion was applied at the polling-stations.

'Such an election cannot be considered as representative of the will of the electorate and cannot therefore be regarded as genuine. It must be annulled and, after first establishing the conditions necessary for free voting, held again.

'I intended to present my protest before the courts but a careful study of the present laws governing elections led me to the disheartening conclusion that a denunciation cannot be made through judicial channels. For example:

'Law 2.015 of 28.5.1946 and the Decree 37.570 of 3.10.1949, which control presidential elections, make the following provisions regarding appeals:

'—Petitions may be made against illegality of electoral procedure, but only in relation to the polling-station where the petitioner exercises the right to vote;

'—The elections will be considered as null and void only when, such illegality being confirmed, the said illegality could affect the overall result of the polling;

'—If the election be annulled, it shall be held again in the polling-station in question.

'This means that the law allows individual protests which can make no substantial impression on the election, but does not allow the election as a whole to be attacked, even if, as in the present case, the whole procedure is nothing but one huge fraud, fragmented into lesser frauds throughout almost all the polling-stations.

'The Political Constitution of the Republic declares expressly in Article 17 that: "Sovereign power resides in the nation, whose most highly representative constituent is the President of the Republic."

'Section 3 of the same Article confirms that the nation is the Portuguese people, for it states that: "The Nation is composed of all Portuguese citizens resident inside or outside Portuguese territory."

'Moreover, the Universal Declaration of Human Rights, which today constitutes Portuguese internal law, both through Article 4 of the Constitution and by our entry into the U.N., prescribes in Paragraph 3 of Article 21 that: "The will of the people shall be the basis of the Government's authority and shall be expressed in periodical and genuine elections which shall be by universal and equal suffrage and held by secret vote or similar free voting procedures."

'And Article 30 of the same Declaration states: "Nothing in this Declaration may be interpreted as implying for any state, group or person any right to engage in any activity or to perform any action aimed at the destruction of any of the rights and freedoms set forth herein."

'When they are not genuine, as they certainly were not in this case, the value of the elections is nil, for the results do not correspond to the will of the electorate, and the President so elected is not the legitimate representative of the nation, which does not want him, but merely of the Government that installed him. Only Your Excellency, the present President of the Republic, can redress the affront and violence enacted upon the nation. So I appeal to Your Excellency to hold new presidential elections which must be genuine and honest. Your Excellency has the constitutional and other necessary powers at your disposal to do this.

'Therefore, both as an individual and as a representative of the nation, I appeal to Your Excellency to:

'*a*) Set up a Government which will decree elections and guarantee that they will be honestly and freely held.

'*b*) To create a commission which, in its inquiries, will guarantee impartial consideration of all abuses, violence, irregularities, etc. which have been committed.

Humberto Delgado
General'

Craveiro Lopes replied to this with the following letter on which, no doubt, history will pass its own judgement:

The Office of the President of the Republic.

'Excellency Sr General Humberto Delgado.
'No.863   Proc.o. 8–5951.

'With reference to your letter of 21st instant, I have been charged by His Excellency, Sr President of the Republic, to inform Your Excellency that, as the laws allow for protest against the electoral procedure by judicial means, as stated in Decree 37.569 of 3rd October 1949, and as Your Excellency did not make use of this right, he sees no other means of appeal against the alleged illegality of the elections. Your appeal to the Head of State "to have new elections held" has no legal basis; neither the Political Constitution nor the mandates pertaining to the election of the President of the Republic allows for direct intervention by the Head of State in relation to the initiation of elections.

"We offer Your Excellency our respects.

To the honour of the Nation'

(The signatory was a secretary of some kind.)

Even the number of the decree was incorrect.

What can one do in such circumstances but plot a revolt against the régime? When I did so on 18th December, those taking part failed to appear and, in regard to the one on 12th March, a large number of the conspirators were arrested by P.I.D.E.

CHAPTER XII

My appeal to the generals

THE revolt which should have taken place on 2nd June had misfired and the disgraceful election fraud had occurred, but still the Army slumbered on in comfortable apathy. I did my best to arouse the patriotism of the highest ranking generals. Tomás was to be inaugurated on 9th August and so, two weeks before, I put before the generals a plan for a *coup d'état* which would probably not even entail any violence. But they refused!

Here is my historic letter which, apart from the 'Proclamation to the Portuguese People', is considered by some as the most important document of the whole campaign.

'Lisbon, 27th July 1958

'To Generals: Júlio Botelho Moniz
      Federico Lopes da Silva
      Carlos da Costa Macedo
      José Beleza Ferraz

'Dear Colleagues:

'*Re: The Army at this tragic moment in the history
    of the nation*

'The four addressees, being respectively Chief of General Staff of the Armed Forces, President of the Supreme Military Court, Chief of the General Staff of the Air Force and Chief of the General Staff of the Army, are, together with Admiral Guerreiro de Brito, the highest

131

ranking officers of the Land, Sea and Air Forces and are distinguished by their extra star. I feel therefore that it is to you, Generals, that I should address this letter, appealing to the honour of the Army and, in a wider sense, to the whole of the Armed Forces.

'Although this matter is more directly concerned with the Army, the major military power which organized and carried out the 28th May revolt, I also address myself to General Costa Macedo, Chief of the General Staff of the Air Force, because Aviation, which is now termed as the Air Force, was until a short time ago part of the Army—as I myself have been throughout my service as a cadet and subsequently as Artillery Officer, Pilot Officer and Officer of the General Staff. Of the thirty-six years I have spent in the Services, thirty were in the Army, that is to say, until the Air Force became an independent branch of the Forces.

'I have not included Admiral Guerreiro de Brito, Chief of Staff of the Navy, for various reasons. The most important of these is the fact that Admiral Américo Tomás, whom the Government claim won the elections for the President of the Republic, is also a naval officer and so I feel it wise to leave out this branch of the Forces completely.

'Neither before nor during the electoral campaign have I ever sought support from any of the addressees even though I have been on close and friendly terms with them for years either in the Army School or in the Military College.

'I need give no further explanation, for this letter is intended to deal with the electoral campaign which we wanted to carry through to its conclusion, for the first time in the thirty-two years of dictatorship, believing that our strength lay in the people's support, in spite of the irregularities, brutalities, monstrosities and dishonesty perpetrated by the Government. It is now common knowledge that the votes were not counted but falsified, except in the rare cases where the Government had not given sufficient instructions for their trickery or violence or where there was no one to carry them out.

'I happen to be the victim of one of the worst electoral robberies in history, as I have proved over and over again in the protest I sent to our colleague Francisco Craveiro Lopes, the Air Force officer who, until the 9th of next month, occupies the position of President of the Republic.

'In this document I requested that the Government be dismissed so that new and genuine elections could be held. He did not do this and gave as his excuse the very same Constitution for which the Government he himself has appointed has no respect, denying the nation all the rights listed in Article 8, which form the basic public liberties.

'Meanwhile there were substantial rumours that although Lopes failed to satisfy my request he was nevertheless plotting with generals and other officers along the same lines as my own proposal, just as his predecessor, the deceased General Oscar Fragoso Carmona, had done. The paradoxical situation is repeated for, although the revolution on 28th May was military in character and the President of the Republic a general (for the sake of appearances), he is in fact no more than a puppet who cannot even dismiss a Minister such as Santos Costa.

'The present conspiracy, which on this level would be best called a *coup d'état*, need not have involved actual fighting or penal responsibilities for the generals and troops. The main object was simply to depose the present Defence Minister.

'I do not intend in this letter to state how far the rumours concerning the *coup d'état* are true, but I have been told that those involved have been transferred or even arrested. I was waiting to see how it would turn out, although I did not hope for much. ... The fact is that a short while ago rumour had it that the conspiracy or *coup d'état* had misfired and, seeing 8th August drawing near, I felt that the time was ripe to write to you, for I will not have many more opportunities to use peaceful means to influence either individuals or public organizations.

'I did not decide to write to you while I was still being hounded by a Government which has all the Armed Forces at its disposal and, paradoxically, the support of an Army which, with its generals, detests it; by a dishonest, lying Government which has broken all its promises to the Opposition, for it even went so far as to claim that it would allow freedom of the press and then forbade publication of the photographs of the crowd of 200,000 or so who were waiting to welcome me in Oporto; by a Government who blatantly allowed the cars distributing my ballot-papers to be held up; by a Government which, whilst making it as difficult as possible for me to hold political meetings, paid for coaches and bribed people to fill the halls at the Salazarist assemblies; by a Government which ordered P.I.D.E. to harass me in a completely disgraceful manner, as General Costa Macedo had occasion to state in front of the Under-Secretary of State for the Air Force.

'I tolerated this moral degradation and the bitterness of seeing the blind enthusiasm of the Army and the Air Force, including my fellow generals, but naturally not the civilian employees in the aviation offices at Alverca. I have lived for half a century and am well versed in history, and so I know only too well what life is like, what reactions to expect when someone steps forward out of the crowd, and especially from those who follow the same profession or have been educated in the same schools. Therefore I accept their indifference.

'Now, however, it is no longer simply a matter of a candidature or insults to a general, although these could have and indeed *should* have been the concern of the generals and troops also. I say "should have" not only because of this camaraderie but also because the Opposition showed a special consideration for the Armed Forces by selecting their candidate from among its generals, despite having practically all the civilian intellectuals from which to choose. Moreover, they chose me, not because of the strings I pulled but because of my record and experience; I did not belong to the *aurea mediocritas* which, right from the Army School, is carried along like a dead weight and obtains a generalship only because it has lived long enough or is not old enough to retire.

'No, we are no longer dealing with an individual, but with a nation which by its demonstrations desperately and enthusiastically showed its dissatisfaction with the Government as unmistakably as any plebiscite. Yet the Government and its hired assassins shamefully robbed it of its rights in the elections; as is shown only too clearly in the enclosed document.

'Next, I should like to point out the lack of intelligence of the members of the Government who never thought it possible that a general on the active list should differ from Carmona and Craveiro Lopes to such an extent that he should actually offer himself as an Opposition candidate for the Presidency of the Republic. By this I mean that those Government members considered themselves as owners of the Armed Forces, looking upon them as a private police force, not the property of the nation. That is what every Portuguese civilian says, when he thinks of the hundreds of thousands of contos which the Armed Forces cost him and his fellows, only to be used to keep internal public order, not for their rightful purpose of fighting foreign enemies.

'This disgraceful situation was so firmly established that during the actual electoral campaign the Defence Minister publicly declared that the Armed Forces were backing Admiral Américo Tomás and thus he seemed to treat all the officers, from the generals to the lieutenants, as children, forgetting that the law gives them the right to vote individually. In short, Costa considers that the

Army and the generals belong not to the nation, but to him personally.

'Turning to the subject of my colleagues and supporters who have been insulted, imprisoned and tortured by P.I.D.E., I shall simply say that were it not for the Army's apathy, such treatment could never have taken place. Similarly, it would not have been possible to affront the martyred nation with Decree No. 40,550 of 12th March 1956, by which, as an ultimate insult, any temporary sentence can be commuted into life imprisonment without further trial, by extending it by periods of three years for as long as P.I.D.E. judges the person concerned sufficiently dangerous. It is worth remarking that this decree has been instituted despite Article 8 of the Political Constitution of the Republic which clearly states that there should be no life imprisonment.

'The Army and its generals continue to feign ignorance of these facts and this can only be considered as a deplorable attitude.

'Even the *Folha*, the newspaper of São Paulo, in its edition of the 9th instant, which I obtained despite the great care of P.I.D.E. to ban certain papers, refers to the "medieval régime imposed upon the country by a court of maniacs who rely upon the sword and crosier for the wholesale plunder which they practise". The sword refers, of course, to the generals.

'The French *L'Express* on 12th June of this year published an article on the same lines entitled "The Final Farce", which was their term for the Portuguese elections on 8th June. The writer, after first describing the procedure in this disgraceful fraud, refers to the brutalities practised upon the courageous hero, Henrique Galvão who, at the age of sixty-three has been sentenced to a further sixteen years' imprisonment, although he did no more than the whole nation is doing, even apparently the officers, who however are more cautious; namely he planned to overthrow the hated Government and published pamphlets to this effect. Then it goes on to say:

' "Last Sunday (8th June) however, the apparently static situation did at last change.

' "After thirty years of farce, there suddenly appeared 'a man without fear or dishonour', General Humberto Delgado, the director of Civil Aviation, who resolved to see it through to the end and force the régime to show its hand. The result was 75% of the votes in favour of the régime.

' "Insofar as the actual Constitution is concerned, the farce is now over and probably for the last time, for Salazar has decided to revise the Constitution. In future there will be no risk, as the Head of State will be elected by Parliament where 120 out of 120 deputies are completely loyal to Salazar.

' "The three pillars of the régime—the generals, large property-owners and the clergy—can now sleep in peace until the day when the Portuguese people, who, after thirty years of order, social stability and a balanced budget, still remain the most wretched and ignorant nation in Europe, find a way other than by elections of making themselves heard."

'Finally, this convenient attitude of *laissez faire* on the part of the Portuguese generals causes them to be taunted and scorned in the foreign press. Due to the Army's apathy the country is in the same state as it would be if occupied by a foreign military force, with the sole difference that neither the hermit of Belem nor the Armed Forces have any political power and, through their officers, the latter do no more than perform the most odious of duties by supporting P.I.D.E., the police, the censorship and, basically, acting as the dictator's Praetorian Guard.

'Do you Generals believe that the Portuguese people are such unimportant members of the human race that after eight centuries of history they must be less privileged than the Ghanaians in Africa or the Indians in Asia?

'Do you Generals believe that it is a spirit of patriotism

and self-sacrifice that inspires Salazar and Costa to remain in power? What kind of sacrifice can it be which makes them decide to hold on to their position in spite of the strangled cries of the nation urging them to leave? Moreover, their services are neither free nor cheap as can be seen by comparing the salaries they have received for decades as members of the Government with those they would have obtained if they were still professors at Coimbra or Army officers.

'Do you Generals not know that uniformed officers no longer dare appear in the streets? If they do they have to endure the jibes, or at least the hostile looks, of the civilians.

'I presume that you are not going to consider this letter as the cunning ruse of a comrade who, having no troops at his disposal, since Costa has refused him a military command, is looking to his colleagues for help in attaining the position of President of the Republic. The fact that I openly fought these elections out to their bitter end, despite the treacherous actions such as the armed assault upon the cars distributing my ballot-papers to the people, which I have already described above, should prove that this is not so. Moreover you are aware that neither the nation nor myself would accept the generals' revolt rather than genuine and honest elections. We are old friends and know each other too well to imagine that you are generously and simply going to hand me the post of President of the Republic on a plate. For logical and practical reasons such an hypo-thesis can be put on one side. The most important aspect of the subject is simply the question of the nation.

'You are able, possibly without even bloodshed, to stop this orgy of violence and political dishonesty, for all you need do is to shake off your inertia and acquiescence or relegate your gratitude and loyalty, your friendly rela-tion with Santos Costa to second place. Your obligation is purely subjective, as it is a Minister's duty to choose for positions of responsibility the most capable of the generals, and I imagine that you consider yourself as such. As for your loyalty, everyone should bear in mind that no great deed can be accomplished in this world without some form of treachery, as witness the history of the winning of independence in so many countries. Moreover, from the monarchists' point of view, the Republic itself was an act of treachery and the 28th May revolt was considered treachery by the republicans then in power.

'The fact is that the nation is astounded by the inertia of the Armed Forces who are and will be celebrated in song and story in far from flattering terms.

'If this apathy and inertia were overcome, it would be easy to devise some action or series of actions to prevent the final consummation of the election fraud when, on 9th August, Tomás is prepared to challenge the nation and abjectly obey Dr Salazar who is supported by the Armed Forces which Santos Costa promised him would be on his side—without even consulting their opinion!

'Thus, mindful of the sorrowful state of our country, I, a fellow-general, write to you and am ready to run any risk in order to free it from slavery, although I am living primarily on my reduced salary and have two children to support.

'I shall give just a few examples of how the generals might act, and the details could be arranged at a meeting called by the most senior amongst you who is at present in Lisbon: possibly he could invite certain other generals who have direct command of the troops.

'—A declaration addressed by the generals to the Government, declaring that they do not recognize the elections as having been impartial and, consequently, request that Admiral Américo Tomás should not take office as President of the Republic on 9th August.

'—A protest against the transfer of several officers, including some brought home from Africa, because they either voted for the Opposition or showed their support in other ways.

'—The official resignation of their rank in order to support their declaration and protest; this will symbolize the traditional gesture of surrendering one's sword.

'—An adequate concentration, or at least an alert, of all troops who are ready to fight against the "Costaites", if they are not already aware that the hour of national liberation has arrived, and that this is the moment to save the nation's honour and fulfil the Army's duty towards it.

'There is no need for me to tell you that I am at your disposal to prepare and execute these plans, either alone or with the help of others. I am ready for your summons.

'I do not wish to close this letter without saying how seriously worried I am by the widespread unrest throughout the country. Actually, if this comes to a head without any interference by the Army and solely through the civilians' own measures, the Forces might well find themselves in a similar position to that of the French Army which, after three-quarters of a century, has not yet recovered from its awkward position during the Dreyfus Case. The unfortunate conduct of General Boisdeffre, Chief of the General Staff of the Army at that time, who was later forced to resign, remains sharply engraved on the memory of France as a symbol of injustice and corruption.

'In that affair, the Army and its generals took action against an innocent officer but, in the case of Portugal, the passivity of the Army amounts to taking political action, albeit of a negative kind, against a whole nation, which is an even graver matter.

'Quite naturally, the civilian finds this attitude of the Army, with its traditions of bravery and gallantry, strange and incomprehensible. In fact, on the one hand, the Government resembles a wild but stunned beast in its death-throes, whilst on the other the civilians, unarmed and incapable of any real action, gave a fine example of courage when the Government maliciously and brutally ordered the police force to attack them and even open fire upon them merely because they acclaimed the Opposition candidate.

'I should be most grateful if you would, by return of post if possible, acknowledge receipt of this letter if only with a visiting card or a brief telephone call, so that I can be assured it has arrived safely.

'I should also be grateful for any instructions, comments or suggestions in regard to this letter whose object must be quite clear. I hope that none of you will continue to take refuge behind the excuse that you are not "politicians", for the Army has never been so closely connected with politics as it is at present, having supplied the Government with two members from among yourselves.

'The undersigned is fully aware that the Armed Forces should have nothing to do with politics, as is the case in the great democracies, but this is not the time for such opinions when so many generals on the active list and in positions of command are dabbling in politics all the time and in a very dubious manner.

'My deepest respects.

(signed) Humberto Delgado.

General of the Air Force.'

I shall now describe the results of this letter.

Botelho Moniz simply did not reply—a convenient solution!

Lopes da Silva, bless him, sent a message by word of mouth which is easier, telling me that I was quite right but he could not carry out my suggestions.

C. Macedo, who agreed with Ferraz on several points, answered: 'I cannot agree with your concept of loyalty as you define it in your letter and therefore I must repudiate the suggestions you put forward and regret that I have not the time to comment, as I should like to have done, on the various points you make, but I disagree with most of them and feel that you are exaggerating.'

B. Ferraz, my colleague in the General Staff Course and in the Army School, replied: 'We have different conceptions both of politics and of loyalty, and therefore we cannot meet on the same ground nor follow the same paths.'

It might be thought that these gentlemen were observing regulations or being loyal, but ask the officers, cadets, sergeants, corporals or privates if any one of them was a better professional soldier than myself. As for loyalty, which at times is completely inopportune, every one of them had taken part in the 28th May revolt as I had done.

CHAPTER XIII

The National Independent Movement and the Government's reaction

THE people strongly resented the insolent manner in which they had been deprived of real elections, and of the wholesale imprisonment of those who had done no more than show their lack of confidence in, or hatred of, the Government. However, the authorities did not hesitate for a moment but called in P.I.D.E., their most terrifying weapon, in order completely to destroy any opposition which had already begun to weaken now that contact with its leaders was not possible.

As for myself, I had already decided never to give up the fight either with my pen or my sword and so I continued to write and at the same time plan a military revolt, in spite of the failure of the one prepared for 2nd July. This time people would not, as in former elections, simply return home afterwards to wait patiently for the next one. In a word, this time we would not lay down our arms.

Therefore on 18th June, ten days after the elections, I summoned the national and local representatives in order to organize a definite party, although it was a foregone conclusion that the Government would not allow its existence. We were legally entitled to use the Opposition headquarters for a few more days as we had paid the rent for it, but the police would not permit us to meet there and so we accepted 'S's' offer to use his house, and I am very grateful for this. It was not easy to fit so many people into the private house of someone who lived, and still does live, very modestly—especially since many of Dr Arlindo Vicente's friends also came along.

The atmosphere was electric, for some of the more important of my supporters did not get on very well with those of the ex-candidate. Yet, such are the changes that constantly occur in politics that as the years passed, some of these became my colleague's closest friends.

At this meeting we agreed to create a party called the National Independent Movement, its policies to be based upon the proclamation I had issued to the country at the start of my campaign as the National Independent candidate. My staff were to set out these policies in logical order and plan the organization. However, our work was retarded by the difficulties we encountered in holding meetings and also by the constant travelling to and fro. Due to the various principles involved it was not easy to find a basic definition of the party, but eventually the following was agreed upon:

'The National Independent Movement is a civil organization of individuals, not groups, and has as its immediate objects those put forward during his candidature by General Humberto Delgado, together with express provisions for the raising of the cultural and economic standards of the Portuguese people. It is opposed to all dictatorial or totalitarian concepts and to the inclusion in its own organization of any group, sect or party.'

Later, in a circular from the secretariat, it was stated: 'The candidature of General Humberto Delgado was supported by a National Consultative Committee which included persons of the highest rank and reputation. Since the candidature is now replaced by the National Independent Movement, this committee will be retained and whilst respecting the basic principles of the Movement it will be enlarged as circumstances may require.'

On the day after the Movement had been created I sent the Minister of the Interior a letter of which the following is an extract:

'The elections were carried out in such an abnormal manner and preceded and accompanied by such astonishing irregularities and acts of violence that one is forced to conclude that under the normal procedure of democratic, progressive countries the Opposition would have been the victors. It is impossible to understand how such a movement can be denied recognition as a powerful instrument of public opinion.'

I then informed him of the formation of the Movement and went on:

'For the record, I should like to inform Your Excellency and announce to the nation that:

'*a*) Since more than sufficient proof exists of the irregularity of the procedure, the results of the elections will be refuted by various lawful methods.

'*b*) Moral and financial support will be organized for the victims of repression and demands will continue to be made for the liberation of political prisoners.

'*c*) The right to organize the Movement and hold meetings will be reasserted as well as the freedom to fight for the institution of democratic liberties.

'Meanwhile we shall carry on in the hope that the Government will make a straightforward acknowledgement of the Movement's right to exist, and consequently will enable it to conduct its activities under more liberal and efficient conditions than have hitherto been possible.'

As we expected, the Minister refused permission, hoping thereby to lull us into inactivity.

The Duchess of Braganza

The next day after the election I received a visit from Dona Maria Pia de Saxe Coburg, the legitimate daughter of Carlos I who had been assassinated in 1908. She had come up from Rome and had already made one call upon my wife. She is a charming and liberal-minded woman, and I told her that although I was a republican and therefore opposed to the Monarchy, I could nevertheless envisage a Portugal which she could enter freely. I added that I sympathized with her position, for she had been deprived of her rights and had had to come to my house disguised in dark glasses. I said that in *our* democracy there would be no need for that.

As I write this, the Princess has just had an interview with *La Suisse* of Geneva, in which she attacked Dr Salazar whom she too had looked upon at first as a Messiah. However, she changed her mind when she returned to Portugal during the electoral campaign and saw so much misery, tuberculosis and illiteracy under his harsh, unrelenting régime. In this shamefully poor country, she had not even had the satisfaction of seeing the palaces, such as the Carrancas in Oporto or the Vila Viçosa, converted into hospitals.

Faced with the misappropriation of the fortune of her brother, Don Manuel II, who was deposed in 1910 by the Republican Government, she decided to claim her rights which she found had been passed to Don Duarte Nuno, a foreign descendant through Don Miguel of the Absolutist branch, which had been banished from the country a century before. She considers herself the rightful Duchess of Braganza and, in a memorandum which she gave the delegates at a meeting in Geneva in May 1961, called to deal with the Laos problem, she claimed their support for her cause.

The Government were so distrustful of me that on 19th June they prohibited me from flying and so took away any excuse I might have had for talking to my friends on the air-fields. Moreover, I was told of an order in a confidential circular sent to the various bases and barracks by the Defence Minister, Santos Costa, which said that I was to be arrested if I appeared at any of them. Obviously something had leaked out about the revolt planned for 2nd June.

I had vowed that my campaign would still go on and so I 'decreed' national mourning on 1st, 2nd, and 3rd July, as a protest against the nullifying of the election. My daughter, Iva Humberta, who was sixteen years old, went to an examination in deep mourning including a black necklace and earrings. When the professor sourly asked what, in her opinion, was the cause of the decadence of the Portuguese theatre, she came back with a neat retort: 'The censorship.'

In a revue at the Maria Vitoria Theatre, the censor had passed a sketch referring to the three candidates for the Presidency of the Republic—Arlindo Vicente, Tomás and myself. When I arrived at the theatre to see myself portrayed by Humberto Madeira, the people burst into wild applause even though the theatre was full of P.I.D.E. agents. It was a very difficult moment but I managed to get out without any nasty incidents.

My notes recall the serious pre-revolutionary activity in which I took part. On 29th May, Captain Romba was arrested on the charge that he had been a liaison officer for the revolt planned for 2nd June. On the same day I received a promise of support from a colonel who, being in Africa, had dared to show his allegiance openly. Unfortunately he had no troops under his command at the time and was not given any. There was plenty of talk but no regiment would start the ball rolling.

On the other hand, the people showed great courage which at least was some consolation. Wherever I went crowds came to welcome me; in Cela, Alcobaça, which I sometimes visited on a Sunday, the 'pilgrimage' assumed such proportions that the National Republican Guard eventually intervened and barred all roads. Yet Cela was little more than a village.

The new Government

Admiral Tomás took office on 9th August and on the 14th he, or rather Salazar, appointed the new Government. Santos Costa was not included in it and his place was taken by General Botelho Moniz whom I had known for thirty years. Although he was some six years younger than I, we had been colleagues in the Military College and the General Staff Course, for this is taken both by the officers of the Army and of the Air Force.

On 3rd September Botelho Moniz summoned me to see him, in his capacity as Minister of Defence but, as I expected, our conversation was rather vague. Briefly, the object of the meeting was to persuade me to cut down my political activity by offering me a commission and consequently a return to my full salary.

The attempt to buy my silence

The whole scandalous affair became known on 22nd September. General Costa Macedo, Chief of Staff for the Air Force, told me that the Government wanted to exile me by sending me on a mission to the United States or Canada, first to find out details about the adaptation of airports for jets, and second to study Economic Science. It was made clear that

I was merely to attend courses in this subject and not to take it seriously. I replied that I was indeed thinking of taking indefinite leave and my political colleagues agreed, at a meeting which I called on the 23rd, that I ought to refuse. On the 24th I had another interview with Botelho Moniz which was once more concerned with my studies in Canada. I answered that I would only go if under formal military orders. Obviously, they wanted to get rid of me quickly.

The troops were not prepared to revolt and so reluctantly I realized that I should have to leave. Therefore I decided to write to two friends of mine in New York—Miss C., an American, and Mrs. W., an Englishwoman. (Since they might have to come to Lisbon one day, it is better not to give their names.) They contacted the *New York Times* and gave my letters to the editor who published extracts from them and condemned the brutality of a military order compelling an officer to study economics against his will. The Government withdrew and on 7th October cancelled the embarkation order. I should like to express my gratitude to the *New York Times*.

Further persecution

The President of the Portuguese Republican Centre in São Paulo, Brazil, Carlos Cruz, invited me to visit his country, but as I was busy planning a military revolt I delayed applying for the necessary military permit until 1st September 1958. My application put the Government in a panic, for how could they refuse me permission to go abroad if I still had no commission and was stuck at home all day? So they cunningly offered me a position from 9th September and then rejected my application on the grounds that I was needed in the Air Force. At the same time Costa Macedo ordered me not to go near the offices of the Under-Secretary of State for the Air Force or have any contact with the officers. In other words I was to remain at home and receive full pay for doing nothing.

A tear-gas attack

On 5th October, the forty-eighth anniversary of the establishment of the Republic, I joined a group which was paying homage to the leading figures of the régime by visiting the tombs of Dr Miguel Bombarda and Admiral Cândido Reis. The procession made its way to the cemetery in a most orderly fashion, but when we came to leave, the police turned awkward and insisted that everyone left through a certain narrow gate. Just as we were about to lay a wreath upon the monument to the late President of the Republic, Dr António José de Almeida, they behaved with indescribable barbarity and attacked us with tear-gas, even though amongst those present were two candidates for the Presidency, Dr Arlindo Vicente and myself, and several elderly members of the Opposition, such as Dr António Sérgio, Dr Jaime Cortesão and Dr Azevedo Gomes. With tears still streaming down my face, I was interviewed by a reporter from the *New York Times* and it is easy to imagine the sort of remarks I made, although words were hardly necessary on this occasion.

Here is how Dr A. Sérgio described the scene to the Minister of the Presidency, Teotónio Pereira:

'When eventually I arrived in the street where the monument to António José de Almeida stands, the people were moving off in a perfectly harmless manner, and some climbed the steps of the statue to place their wreaths. Then, at a certain point in the ceremony, General Humberto Delgado climbed the steps with some of his friends—I cannot say exactly how many, but I should imagine it was about twenty or thirty, which was all there was room for on the steps. When the wreath was placed in position to the applause of those present, Dr Acácio de Gouveia asked them, in the name of the General, to leave quietly, but when they started to move off they were suddenly assailed by tear-gas bombs. Undoubtedly this was an utterly stupid thing to do. As Your Excellency knows, tear-gas is normally only used by the police when they are attacked by a crowd, and so it can only be considered completely irresponsible and idiotic for them to use it on a small group of peaceful citizens who were merely laying wreaths at the foot of a statue.'

A scene with P.I.D.E.

Dr Rodrigo de Abreu invited me to dine that evening at

the Hotel Francfort in the Rua de Santa Justa, right in the centre of Lisbon. As I left the house, I noticed a police car with half a dozen P.I.D.E. members in it suddenly start up and prepare to follow me. I had not felt such an intense hatred for a long time and I asked my wife to take the wheel so that I should be ready for anything that might happen. When we had turned the next corner I asked my wife to stop, and then got out. The P.I.D.E. were obviously embarrassed by this move and stopped as well. I walked towards their car, snatched open the door and told the henchmen that I was going to walk the rest of the way and I should like to see any of them follow me. Meanwhile my wife and daughter went on to the hotel in the car and once I got round the corner, I took a taxi by the Hotel Aviz.

When we were returning late that night, my daughter kept watch out of the back window to see if we were being followed. As we were going up the Avenida Fontes Pereira de Melo, very near my home, she called out: 'Father, they are following us with their lights off!' I quickly spun the car into Edward VII Park but they still kept behind us. I pulled up, blind with anger. My wife was in tears and begged me to take care, but I strode determinedly to their car. With a sudden wrench of the wheel and screaming tyres it sped away into the night.

The Pope

Pope Pius XII died on the 9th and the next day I sent the following telegram to Cardinal Camerlengo:

'Both personally and as Leader of the National Independent Movement, I wish to express sympathy with Your Eminence and the Sacred College of Cardinals for the great loss which the Church has suffered by the death of His Holiness Pius XII, who was admired throughout the world and to whose activities, in both the social and moral spheres, we render our most respectful homage.'

On the 29th, I sent another to Pope John XXIII:

'As Leader of the National Independent Movement, which is striving to secure for the Portuguese people that liberty and respect which the Holy Church of Christ also desires, and on my own behalf, with emotion such as I have seldom experienced before, I should like to assure Your Holiness of our great joy in your elevation to the Throne of St Peter. I should like to add our hope that, strengthened by Your great faith, You will help us to obtain for the Portuguese people tranquillity, peace of mind, happiness and liberation from their constant fear of imprisonment for political reasons.'

The Opposition circulated these telegrams in secret, using the few channels which the police had not yet managed to discover. However, to our great surprise, the telegram found its way into a newspaper but, after a great deal of thought, we realized that this was only a step towards the disciplinary action which they were going to bring against me, for I had publicly avowed myself to be the head of a post-election movement which the Government had refused to authorize.

The Government was extremely annoyed when they realized that the Opposition was not going to knuckle under. On the 12th, someone called Gaspar Queiroz, a friend of Botelho Moniz, came to sound me, assuring me that he did so entirely of his own accord, as to whether I was inclined to go abroad, suggesting that since I had done everything possible, to remain in Portugal would only mean sacrificing myself, and ingloriously at that.

I asked him whether he was aware that the elections were unfair, but he merely replied: 'Oh, come now, they have always been the same.' These words echoed those of Botelho Moniz: for that type of person elections are no more than a formality, a farce. They are held simply to prevent people saying that the Government is totalitarian.

Bevan

In the middle of October the Opposition invited Aneurin Bevan to visit Portugal and give some lectures; this was one way of keeping the 'sacred flame of liberty' burning and of giving the Government a pin-prick. It was common knowledge what Bevan thought of Salazar and in his book, *In Place of Fear*, published by Heinemann, he writes on page 43:

'There are three conceptions of society now competing for the attention of mankind: the Competitive, the Monolithic and the Democratic Socialist. There is a fourth which may be called the Authoritarian Society, after the fashion of Spain and Portugal, but in a curious way these last are not genuine societies at all. They share many of the most repulsive features of the monolithic type without its active genius. They are frozen societies. In so far as they are animated at all, it is by a nostalgia for a romanticized past. ... They reduce the functions of government to an ugly masquerade in which the poverty of their pretensions shows through the tinsel of their ornate façade. They need another Cervantes to blow them into oblivion in a gale of laughter.'

When the Government forbade the visit the Opposition replied:

Lisbon. 11th November 1958

'Mr. Bevan will not be coming here to discuss Portugal's internal problems, but will deal only with subjects of universal interest; therefore any complaints regarding the interference of foreigners in our internal affairs are quite groundless.

'In every country it is usual to employ interpreters to translate lectures given by someone who is speaking in a language which those present do not understand. This is the customary practice in all international conferences whether they deal with politics, science, art or sport, and the Government must be well aware of this.

'... Mme Christine Garnier, the Hitlerites who came here in connection with the Portuguese Youth Movement and all the foreigners invited to explain the thories of the Corporative State have interfered with our political life on former occasions.

'Any claim that Mr Bevan was invited here in order to provoke demonstrations and disturbances of the peace is nullified by the fact that we ourselves informed the Government of our invitation to Mr Bevan and his wife in a letter sent to the Minister of the Presidency on 28th October, and also in one sent to the British Ambassador in Lisbon on the same date.

'This is yet another example of the Government's intention to isolate the country from the general development of contemporary civilization and of their betrayal of the aims set out in the Universal Declaration of Human Rights, especially in Article 19, which was adopted by the United Nations of which Portugal is a member.

'For the Reception Committee:
Humberto Delgado,
Francisco Vieira de Almeida,
Jaime Cortesão,
Mário de Azevedo Gomes,
António Sérgio de Souza.'

On the 15th, the British left-wing magazine, the *New Statesman* wrote: 'Mr Bevan was to have delivered a series of talks on democracy in Portugal. Salazar's régime is theoretically dedicated to such a form of government but it has had great difficulty in convincing the world that it has put it into practice. Their refusal to allow Mr Bevan to go to Portugal is therefore a bad sign and signifies a loss of confidence in the future of the dictatorship. Since General Delgado contested the Presidency of the Republic, nothing has gone right for the Salazar régime. ... In Delgado, Salazar has a young, competent and respectable rival whom no one can accuse of Communism or anti-West or anti-clerical ideas. Above all, the country is today in a constant state of ferment whipped up by the growing conviction that at last something is going to happen.'

On 22nd November P.I.D.E. arrested the four civilians who had signed the document quoted earlier in which we had denounced the Government for not allowing Mr Bevan to visit the country. I was not arrested as I was under military law, but this respite did not last long as we shall see. I felt that I was in an embarrassing position and therefore on 23rd November I sent the Minister of the Presidency, Teotónio Pereira, the following telegram:

'In my telegram of 25th October I protested against the imprisonment of Sr José Moreira de Assunçao of Lisbon, to whom I had given my support. Sr Moreira de Assunçao is however still a prisoner and only allowed to see his wife for a mere quarter of an hour a week.

'On 19th of this month I was the leading signatory of a telegram protesting against the imprisonment of Sr António de Oliveira Valença of Oporto. In this telegram we drew Your Excellency's attention to the wave of terror which is sweeping the country, dominated as it is by the police who seem to be a law unto themselves.

'Yesterday, 22nd November, Srs António Sérgio, Jaime Cortesão, Mário de Azevedo Gomes and Vieira de Almeida were arrested. These men are all in their seventies and have a high intellectual reputation in this country and, moreover, from the political point of view, the first three are republicans and the last a monarchist. They were, like myself, all signatories of our statement to the Government and of other documents concerning the visit of Mr A. Bevan to Portugal.

'I am not aware of the reasons for their arrest by P.I.D.E., but in face of such an infamous happening I claim, as the leading signatory of these documents, not only a common cause with these prisoners but the chief responsibility.

'. . . It is hard to understand how the Government can find any enjoyment in their determination to reduce themselves to governing nothing but concentration camps and cemeteries.'

On 2nd December, the Government behaved even more basely. On that day my son, Humberto Delgado (Humberto II), a captain in the Air Force, was to be married, and naturally everything was rather chaotic. The ceremony was planned for 11 a.m. and shortly before, I had telephoned my secretary, telling her to come and see me afterwards in order to pick up some letters and deliver them. I was well aware that my phone was tapped by the police and therefore made sure that she would only be carrying letters of secondary importance.

When she left me she was arrested by P.I.D.E. and made to spend some six or seven hours in their office, while they took all the correspondence in her possession away from her and kept it for a considerable time; some of my papers including my address book, are still in their hands.

I was so completely ashamed of and incensed by this high-handed behaviour that on the 3rd I sent a strong complaint to the Defence Minister, General Botelho Moniz:

'Yesterday one of my employees, carrying some of my correspondence, was detained at 11.30 while leaving my house, taken to P.I.D.E.'s offices and kept there and interrogated for nearly seven hours. Some documents I had written were seized, including papers of a purely private nature and also the instructions I had given her regarding her day's duties. Apart from this, the police appropriated the mail she was to deliver and kept it for nearly three hours, which is far longer than is needed merely to read the names of the addressees. This means that whatever I write is liable to be read by any officer of P.I.D.E. under the command of an Army captain although, according to the Constitution, my letters should be inviolable. Thus I am treated as if I were guilty of some public offence instead of being one of Your Excellency's colleagues.

'. . . If your Excellency, as a member of the Government, is really unable to protect me, as your subordinate and one time colleague, against these insults, I beg you to tell me so straight out so that should I use my own methods to defend myself it will not be taken as unorthodox or irregular.

'It could well happen that in the course of some future involvement with P.I.D.E., they might kill me on the pretext that it was done in self-defence. Therefore it seems sensible for me to pass on this suspicion to Your Excellency in order to ensure that, even if the Armed Forces are not concerned by the insults to one of their generals, at least my family will know that I warned Your Excellency beforehand and will also know on what grounds they must make their claim for justice, both to those in authority and to History.'

It is possible that in spite of all I have described here there are still some influential people in Brazil who continue to look upon Dr Salazar as a saint. There are none so deaf as those that will not hear.

Under this tension I, as the weaker of the parties, was bound to be broken and this is how it happened.

On 26th November the Government announced my fate in the following official bulletin:

'Drs Jaime Cortesão, António Sérgio de Souza, Professors Mário de Azevedo Gomes and Francisco Vieira de Almeida have been detained for questioning. These arrests have been made because the above have signed subversive manifestos which have been distributed in secret. General Humberto Delgado's signature also appears on some of these manifestos and both for this and his other well-known activities, an action is being brought against him by the Under-Secretary of State for the Air Force.'

This was the culmination of a devilish plan designed to plunge me into complete misery. As a pilot I had flown but when the cockpit was forbidden I had become in turn a horseman, mounted on the Government's back, goading it with my spurs, then a pedestrian, trailing my troubles on foot through Lisbon, and then an armchair general, having been refused permission to go to work, and now they intended to have me flat on my back like a statue by depriving me even of the means to vegetate.

CHAPTER XIV

Arrest, asylum and exile

THE accusations brought against me were all of a political nature, based upon the Protest against the Elections, a letter I wrote to Admiral Tomás refusing to congratulate him on his victory, the creation of the National Independent Movement and, amongst other things, even upon various official documents which General Botelho Moniz had accepted, thus giving them a legal status, and removing any taint of irregularity.

On 4th December Esquivél, the general in charge of the inquiry, summoned me. He was embarrassed and we shook hands coldly, whilst he avoided my eyes as he presented me with no less than twenty-two questions. In order not to prolong my account, I shall not quote this first version of the questionnaire for the document in which I declared that I was not prepared to answer the questions, but merely say that as a result of my refusal Esquivél immediately modified the wording in the inquiry of 12th December 1958, which I give in full below:

'*Question 1*: Does Your Excellency admit to having written a letter dated 18th July last and addressed to His Excellency the Minister of the Interior in which, apart from references to the electoral procedure, you assumed the position of leader of a political movement called the "National Independent Movement"?

'*Answer*: Yes. I merely object to the term "leader". I prefer "representative".

'*Question 2*: Does Your Excellency admit to having written the pamphlet entitled "A Protest against the Presidential Elections by Candidate General Humberto Delgado", dated 21st June 1958?

'*Answer*: Yes.

'*Question 3*: Does Your Excellency admit to having written the letter dated 23rd June 1958 and sent to His Excellency Admiral Américo Tomás?

'*Answer*: Yes.

'*Question 4*: Did Your Excellency promote or allow the circulation of a pamphlet entitled "The National Independent Movement continues to fight for the Opposition", dated June last, which contains the text of the letter cited in Question 1, as well as instigations to engage in a struggle against the Government, which struggle was termed as "national liberation"?

"*Answer*: I am, as I have said, the writer of that letter. As for 'circulation', I shall not answer that for, couched in such vague terms, the practice of circulating papers of that type might even be attributed to some members of the Government, for who in these days has not passed on a pamphlet or two to someone else?

'Regarding the accusation of "promoting circulation" as opposed to "allowing circulation", I must point out that it is difficult to answer that, for we are in a country where:

'—P.I.D.E. confiscates, and moreover is using as evidence in this trial, a confidential letter of mine which they could easily have published and accused me of circulating;

'—It is said that *Avante*, the organ of the Communist Party, is, occasionally at least, written by P.I.D.E. itself in order more effectively to justify its existence;

'—Several people have assured me that during the electoral campaign the P.I.D.E. cars which were trailing me were distributing pamphlets attacking the National Independent Candidate within a few yards of him!

'As for "allowing circulation", it is difficult to see how circulation can be prevented, especially in a country where the censorship of the press causes the people in their desire for the truth to copy anything that comes to hand. A typical example is the letter of the Rt. Revd. The Bishop of Oporto which, as every one knows, was not personally circulated by His Lordship. I think that explains the situation.

'*Question 5*: Did Your Excellency promote or allow the circulation of a work entitled "An Open Letter from General Humberto Delgado to the New Government" and dated 22nd August 1958, in which a letter addressed by Your Excellency to the Ministers was reproduced?

'*Answer*: My answer is the same as to Question 4, *mutatis mutandis*. The open letter referred to was written by me.'

Questions 6–13 referred to a letter of protest which I had written to the Defence Minister; the letters I wrote to the two ladies in America who passed them on to the *New York Times*; my statement to the same newspaper about having been attacked by tear-gas; a warning I was given to desist from any further political activity, although my Protest against the Elections was in the offing; a question as to whether I regarded such orders as official; a statement to the *New York Times* regarding the idyllic exile in Canada which I was offered; the telegram I had sent as Leader of the National Independent Movement to Cardinal Camerlengo on the death of the Pope, and a letter regarding political affairs sent to the Minister of the Interior.

My answer to all these questions was 'yes'.

'*Question 14*: Does Your Excellency admit to having sent a confidential note, ref. 109, on 20th October 1958, to Srs Vieira de Almeida, Artur Andrade, Moreira de Asuncão, Cunha Leal, António Sérgio and Arlindo Vicente?' (Note: I have given these names in alphabetical order.)

'*Answer*: Yes. I must point out once again that a photocopy of this confidential note is being used in these proceedings and, as none of the recipients would think of passing the letter on to P.I.D.E., I leave it to the generals and others taking part in this case to draw their own conclusions from this sadly typical fact.

'*Question 15*: Does Your Excellency confirm the information sent in a telegram on 24th October 1958, by the Lisbon correspondent of the American newspaper *New York Times*, which states that Your Excellency has on his table at home a Luger revolver loaded with ten bullets which he intends to use against anyone who attempts to arrest him, and that his comment is "If they want war, they can have it"?

'*Answer*: There is normally on the hall-table at home a revolver loaded with ten bullets. There are various eventualities in which its use may be envisaged, including any provocation or violence to which P.I.D.E. might unlawfully subject me. I cannot verify the exact terms which I used to the correspondent of the *New York Times*, but the ones you have given are basically correct and I take full responsibility for them.'

Questions 16–20 concerned the letter sent to Dr Júlio Mesquita Filho and published on 26th October 1958 in *O Estada de São Paulo*; the letter to the Minister of the Interior, requesting permission for Mr Aneurin Bevan to enter the country; a circular calling for contributions towards the welcome for Mr Bevan; a telegram to Pope John XXIII in which I refer to myself as the Leader of the National Independent Movement; and my remarks upon the Government's refusal to allow Mr Bevan to visit the country.

My answer to all these was 'yes'.

'*Question 21*: Does Your Excellency admit to having given an interview to the *Daily Mail*, published on 12th of this month, in which you make various statements such as: "We shall even use guns to get what we want"?

'*Answer*: The interview was not put on record and it is therefore difficult to confirm whether I did in fact use the exact expression quoted. The reporter has nevertheless conveyed the essence of my view, which happily is shared by many of my colleagues; until the country entered its present state of moral degradation, it was also shared by several others who today occupy well-paid positions.

'*Question 22*: Does Your Excellency admit to having written the letter dated 23rd instant and sent to His Excellency the Minister of the Presidency, which protests and inveighs against the Government for ordering certain persons to be imprisoned and which contains the sentence: "It is hard to understand how the Government can find any enjoyment in their determination to reduce themselves to governing nothing but concentration camps and cemeteries"?

'*Answer*: Yes. I regret that you do not ask for proof of this statement. Should the Armed Forces not show some concern about this, since they are paid by the nation to enable it to live like other civilized peoples, rather than to add to its mental and physical tortures?'

With this inquiry, which sealed my fate as far as the Armed Forces were concerned, I concluded my answers to the questionnaire.

On 7th January 1959, I was dismissed from the services. This shameful sentence is rarely imposed and then only in the case of officers who have committed serious moral offences, for it is so severe that the officer can no longer wear his uniform, in contrast to those retired or on the reserve list. Moreover, had I been in either of these categories, the dictator would have had to keep me on almost full pay, thanks to my length of service and the allowance attracted by my years as a pilot but, by dismissing me from the services altogether, he was entitled to pay me anything from nil to 75% of my salary. Yet he actually declared that he was being extremely generous in allowing me the maximum pay that the law permitted! One has to have some acquaintance with military law to find one's way through such complexities.

Let me add that this sentence forbids the carrying of firearms, which no doubt was a relief for P.I.D.E. who could thus pronounce me subversive in a tribunal, simply because I carried a weapon. Also, I would in future be subject to civil law.

In an official statement on the 8th, the dictator could not

hide his true feelings and declared that the military sentence was independent of any other criminal offences of which I might be guilty.

On 12th January 1959 I sought asylum in the Brazilian Embassy in Lisbon. My decision to do so was totally unexpected, for the right of asylum had long since lapsed in Portugal. I therefore infuriated and disconcerted the dictator, with the consequences which I shall now describe.

I shall revert for a moment to the revolt planned for the 18th December 1958, just twenty-four days before I sought asylum. This seems an appropriate point to mention this because it is one of the factors which led me to do so. Moreover, I have just received from Sr Plácido Barbosa, who has a reliable memory, certain details which he has given me permission to use here under his own name and that of his cousin Dr R. de Abreu, who is a member of the family which writes for the Lisbon paper, *República*.

On the morning of the 18th, I had everything ready for the revolt which was planned for that night, but suddenly, a bare twelve hours before the deadline, Manuel Serra came to tell me that it was all off. Through P. Barbosa, I tried to get this tragic news to Oporto, where the liaison officer was R. de Abreu. (Naturally, wherever possible, the liaison work was in the hands of civilians, who were less likely to be suspected by P.I.D.E. in their contacts with military officers.)

Salazar had made his attitude towards me quite obvious and therefore Captain Almeida Santos, one of the chief revolutionaries who had been with us since the revolt planned for 2nd June 1958, insisted on behalf of all the officers in the conspiracy that I must not get caught by the police. On Saturday, 10th January 1959, whilst dining with Dr António Sérgio, I was told that they had heard through the wife of a P.I.D.E. agent that I was in danger of being taken prisoner, and therefore it would be wise to seek asylum in an embassy or hide in a private house. However, I did not pay much attention to this.

I should like to quote what Plácido Barbosa says about this:

'Sérgio invited Your Excellency, Rodrigo de Abreu and myself to his house, since Vidal and Sertório were away, and at dinner we discussed the suggestion that Your Excellency should seek political asylum. Afterwards, we accompanied Your Excellency home, but when we came to see you at 11 a.m. the next morning, we could not find you. We then called on Cunha Leal and told him of Your Excellency's plan to take refuge in the Brazilian Embassy. . . .

'About 2 p.m. we went to your house again and, finding you there, explained that we had heard from Arlindo Vicente that a demonstration had been planned outside your house for the next day, 12th January.

'In the evening, R. de Abreu left by train for Oporto and, after seeing him off, I returned to the house of Cunha Leal who advised me to tell Your Excellency to do your utmost to escape. . . .

'About 10 p.m. I went back to see Your Excellency who had been talking to Montalvão; apparently he had told you that the revolt would not take place and you were completely downcast.

'The next day I received a telephone call at 8 a.m. from R. de Abreu who told me that I must convince Your Excellency to seek asylum in the Brazilian Embassy that very day and so, at 9 a.m., I came to see you and spent an hour trying to persuade you to go to the Brazilian Embassy immediately. . . .

'At 11 a.m. R. de Abreu returned from Oporto by plane, but I did not meet him at the airport because P.I.D.E. were there. Therefore I returned to your house about midday and found "O.S." there. . . . We discussed once more the advisability of your seeking asylum.'

At this point I should like to include a few of my own remarks.

Maria Iva, my wife, hearing the heated discussion, came in and declared that as a wife and mother 'she too had the right to vote', and in her opinion I should definitely seek asylum, for she saw only too clearly the danger I was in.

In this tense atmosphere I explained my own plan of action and announced that I was not going to the Embassy until I had had my hair cut! Since, being so well known, I had asked the barber to come to my house and he would not arrive until after lunch, it was agreed that I should not make the request for asylum until about 3 p.m. The demonstration to cover P.I.D.E.'s attempt to kill or arrest me would not take place before 6 p.m. and so I had plenty of time. It is an amusing and extraordinary coincidence that Amadeu, the barber, while cutting my hair, should himself insist upon my seeking refuge in the Embassy. How can I convince this humble friend of mine that it was not through his efforts that I decided to do so?

P. Barbosa continues:

'We set out for the Embassy and, as we went right around the block containing Your Excellency's house in the Rua Felipe Folque, we noticed that the P.I.D.E. agent stationed at the garage door went inside to phone to headquarters the news of your Excellency's departure. We went straight to Rua António Maria Cardoso. (The Ambassador wasn't there.) Almost immediately "O.S." got involved in an argument with a traffic policeman and this could easily have given P.I.D.E., who had seen us, time to catch us up and possibly arrest us. We then proceeded to the Brazilian Chancellery.

'I left to tell your wife what had happened as soon as we knew that Your Excellency had been granted asylum.

'. . . When I returned to the Brazilian Embassy, Álvaro Lins had already left Rodrigo de Abreu and "O.S.".

'. . . Álvaro Lins has told me here in Brazil that he did not know I had accompanied you to the Embassy.'

When, with a lively step and a cheerful air, the charming Ambassador, Álvaro Lins, entered the Chancellery on his return from the airport, where he had just seen off his colleague, Chateaubriand, the Brazilian Ambassador to London, I explained my position to him.

A few hours later the Ambassador was summoned for interview by Marcelo Matias and told the latter of the bombshell which was to explode in the *dolce far niente* world of the Lisbon diplomatic corps. Only then could I be taken from the Chancellery to the Embassy where I was to be lodged. Other writers have not sufficiently stressed this humane and manly decision of Álvaro Lins, which would have done credit to a general. However, I shall not go into details here, for his excellent book, *Mission in Portugal*, deals with this affair and he will go into it again in his second volume. I shall merely say that, as I expected from the first, Lins became very much sought after at international social gatherings, to give his version of what had happened.

When at last I was safely installed and in possession of extra-territorial rights, I thrilled with delight and felt a surge of new strength at the prospect of being in a free country. It was balm to my weary mind to enjoy the company of the charming and cultured D. Heloísa and her children, pretty Teresa, and Pedro who, with his revolutionary inclinations, was also a sturdy 'Delgadisto'.

Yet, at the same time, I felt a strange sensation for one who had travelled to the four corners of the earth. Could I abandon everything and go to a foreign country, with no profession nor funds to support myself? Could I take a blind leap into the unknown, forsaking rank, family, friends and a lifetime's achievement now, at the peak of my career? After the exultation of escaping Salazar's gang came the natural reaction. I felt a chilly depression envelope me like a cold sweat in the face of my surrender to the unknown. It was a solemn moment as my hearty laughter met icy inward forebodings.

The documents I handed to the Embassy

On my first day, 12th January, I presented the Ambassador with 'Memo No. 1', which began: 'I sought asylum today on the grounds of coercion and imminent imprisonment.' In this document I took the opportunity of showing the Brazilian Government just how little the Portuguese Government could be trusted. On the 8th, they had announced that I had been punished according to military regulations 'independently of offences of a criminal nature for which he might still be held responsible'. Yet now, four days later, they showed their scorn both for the Portuguese people and human intelligence, by stating in the *Diário Popular* that no one was persecuting or attacking me or restricting my movements. My position had been effectively defined by the decision of the Under-Secretary of Aviation and the matter was now closed.

By the 13th, the dictator had thought the matter over more carefully and issued a more amicable statement. Apparently he was beginning to realize the full strength behind the blow I had dealt him and which roused him from the numbness of his sedentary life and the delusions of thirty years of power. He said that he had no intention of having me arrested for the offences which I had committed up to that time. How could he have, if no civil action had yet been brought against me?

The dictator went on to say that if he had had any intention of arresting me, he would have had a sentence of imprisonment passed, and not the 'benevolent' sentence which merely removed me from the services and reduced me to three-quarters of my salary! At this point I should mention that in a second disciplinary action I was dismissed and lost all my salary.

In my second memo to the Ambassador I added: 'The more the Government talk about me the more careful I have to be never to take what they say at its face value. . . . Although their behaviour in the past makes it unlikely, if in fact the Government is not opposed to my leaving the country, I cannot understand why they do not help me by practical means to obtain the necessary documents immediately, without my having to risk an incident engineered by P.I.D.E. This hated police force has destroyed so many of my compatriots that they are naturally afraid of anyone coming to power who would call them to account. So they would be much easier in their minds if I were killed or imprisoned. After any clash with them I would, of course, get the blame and the Government would claim that I was no longer covered by any agreement.'

In my third memo, referring to my departure for Brazil, I said: 'This will be carried out in the manner which His

Excellency the Brazilian Ambassador has already stated in public and in the press, guaranteeing me his protection as far as the airport or place of embarkation.'

As to the possibility of my leaving the Embassy as a 'free citizen', I stated that in that case I should no longer wish to go to Brazil.

Henrique Galvão

The enthusiasm aroused in the country by my electoral campaign gave rise to unusual happenings: a stream of political refugees and prison escapes including that of Henrique Galvão; the restlessness which was evident in the communications addressed to the Government and in the hundreds of secret pamphlets; and the constant references to the Opposition in the foreign press, so much so that more articles about us were published in one year than in the thirty preceding years. The spectacular flight of Henrique Galvão from a hospital to a private house and then later to the Argentine Embassy once more called attention to this man who had been closely associated with Dr Salazar in many capacities, but had since broken with him completely.

Captain Galvão is ten years older than myself and belongs to the generation of the 'cadets' of Sidónio Pais (1918), a period I have described in an earlier chapter. He was not promoted beyond the rank of captain, since in his age-group the upper ranks were filled by Infantry subalterns and therefore he opted for civilian posts.

He was thirty years old in 1926, when the military dictatorship was set up and so he was naturally one of those who were able to take advantage of the normal custom of distributing offices to those most closely involved in the conspiracy. In this way he became Governor of Huíla, a district in Angola, director of the National Broadcasting Company and head of various missions. Understandably, his former colleagues in the Army became jealous when they saw him, while still so young, holding civil posts whose salary was equivalent to that of a general. Therefore they took a grim pleasure in exploiting the youthful prank he had been guilty of a few years before while still an officer in the Infantry Training School, when he had made off with the doors of a chapel in the Convent of Mafra, in which the school was garrisoned. As he belonged to the Infantry and had then followed a civil career, it is not surprising that we had met only about a dozen times between 1926 and 1952.

In 1952, when I was a colonel, he was arrested and charged with plotting against the régime. People were surprised when I visited him in prison and offered to act as witness at his trial, an offer which he nobly refused since, as I have explained, this would have meant that I would lose my generalship. When I was in Washington we wrote to each other in spite of the censorship and when I passed through Lisbon on my return to Europe I visited him once more. This aroused great public interest and meant much embarrassment for P.I.D.E., for they had to authorize visits made by the Head of the Military Mission to N.A.T.O.

In this way our friendship grew until one day, seeing that no officer on the active list visited him and that he was completely alone, I suggested that in future we used the familiar 'tu' and thus our relationship became even closer. So I was perfectly acquainted with every detail of his plan to escape from hospital and I was the person who advised him to choose the Argentine Embassy; he escaped on 16th January 1959, four days after I had sought asylum, and entered the Argentine Embassy on 17th February.

The Opposition's ingenuousness

I was greatly surprised to learn on 18th January that that fine man, Dr Arlindo Vicente, who had been a candidate for the Presidency until he withdrew in my favour, still believed the promises of the Portuguese Government. He prepared a document in which it was proposed that I should stay in the country if I received the Government's guarantee that I would not be molested.

Dr António Sérgio very kindly called a press conference to defend me from the Government's accusations, but the Government prohibited its being held.

On the 20th, Marcelo Matias, the Minister for Foreign Affairs, began to do his utmost to convince the Ambassador that I should be allowed out 'free' from the Embassy. First of all I was to go and have tea in the Chiado and then take a leisurely stroll to the offices of the Civil Government in Lisbon and then to the Under-Secretary of Aviation in order to make the necessary applications. Afterwards I was to go home where no one would disturb me and, after a few days, like a good middle-class citizen, I would go to the airport to catch a plane to Brazil. It seemed so simple, but he did not mention that he intended to surround me with a battery of photographers and reporters who would thus show the world how idiotic I was to imagine a danger that did not exist. Presumably Álvaro Lins, who had believed me, would also be made to look a fool.

Matias slowly reduced the conditions until finally he said that I need only spend a few minutes at home to make out the papers and then hand them in at the last moment at the airport. However, he absolutely refused to agree when I insisted that I must be accompanied by a diplomat in order to show that I was under the protection of a foreign power. Naturally it did not matter whether I left the Embassy for a week, a day or even an hour, for just one second was enough to make me lose my rights of asylum.

Life at the Embassy

I remember with warmth and affection the days I spent with the hospitable Lins family. I did my best to make myself invisible and not to intrude, so as not to disturb them, but they would not let me. 'Come and watch television, General'; 'Have a little more of this Brazilian meat' (dried meat, a novelty and a treat to me), and so on.

Lins, who had literary talents, was inclined to turn night into day and when I realized that the supremely thoughtful D. Heloísa always came to lunch alone, I gave up this meal and made my breakfast more substantial, as the English do. Even so, it alarmed me to see how my waist-line was expanding until it nearly equalled my chest measurement. I began to worry at the sight of my figure threatening to take on the usual contours of Portuguese generals.

Various groups of Portuguese showed their appreciative feelings towards the Ambassador and his wife by writing their thanks and sending bouquets. The women, too, did not fail to pay their respects to the Ambassadress, and my family came to visit me every day. A few friends passing in the street waved to me and I acknowledged them discreetly with the faintest bow from the window. Often I thought how simple it would be to communicate with the outside world by means of a heliograph and the Morse Code.

The pernicious Portuguese press

Almost without exception the press attacked or maligned me and on 28th January, the Lisbon *Diário de Notícias* raised a matter which has since become proverbial, namely the fine example of those Brazilian refugees who, when in Portugal, never speak ill of their Government and always show discretion. The complete hypocrisy of this showed that the writer had been well-trained by the Salazarists. Like certain Brazilian newspapers who were probably paid to keep quiet, he did not mention that if these refugees had spoken out, they would have quickly been escorted to the frontier, for basically both régimes were similar. On the other hand in Brazil the majority of people showed an extraordinary understanding and sympathy.

Maria Iva

Since I was a poor officer, with the same house as when I was a lieutenant, on a reduced salary which was quite liable to be stopped altogether, someone suggested that the Portuguese people should present me with a house. I was told this by a friend in the Opposition, who added with the most honest and puritanical air imaginable that he had quashed the idea from the beginning by saying that I did not want tips. Yet, oddly enough, it was almost a tradition that any pilot who made an occasional flight to Africa received presents.

Another notable incident was Dr Salazar's decision, after hearing rumours of a conspiracy, to give the civil and military officials a rise. The captains, the essential elements for a successful revolution, received an extra 900 escudos a month, whilst the generals only received 1,000. Salazar's tactics were only too obvious, but the people were delighted. They wrote to me to express their gratitude for my having indirectly caused this improvement in the standard of living of thousands of civil servants. It was suggested that I should be given a present and every official was to subscribe one day's salary. One day, with great amusement, I showed Lins the result of this suggestion, for one solitary lady with touching naïvety had sent me her contribution of 50 escudos. What a sacrifice this must have been for the poor woman and how pleased she probably was at the thought of the house I was going to buy!

On 28th February Maria Iva joined in the chorus of national feeling by writing to President Kubitschek to thank him for confirming the asylum granted by Lins. The letter ended: 'Although we deeply feel the absence, both in our hearts and in our house, of the head of the family, there is nevertheless a relative peace of mind in knowing that he is protected by our gallant and hospitable sister-country from further violence and insults.'

Nor, despite her gentle nature, did she omit to protest strongly to Dr. Teotónio Pereira on 14th April about P.I.D.E. having stolen my correspondence: 'In order to get additional proof that my mail is subject to a vexatious and pernicious Gestapo-like censorship, I have written letters to myself which would look suspicious to P.I.D.E. and these have never arrived.' The Minister of the Presidency did not reply and yet they dare to call us free men.

Extracts from my diary

17th February: As a result of clever manoeuvring by Ambassador Rocheta in Rio de Janeiro, Lins called upon me to make an official statement in the presence of some of the secretaries in regard to my present situation. I replied: 'Please telegraph to the Minister, Negrão de Lima, and tell him that I shall leave the Embassy only if I am expelled in writing. Alternatively, I shall seek refuge in Brazil under the terms already offered.'

The end of February: There is a rumour that the revolutionaries do not want me to leave for Brazil until after the date planned for the revolt, 12th March.

2nd March: Erico Vérissimo has given a lecture in the National Theatre, which was greeted by enthusiastic applause. Álvaro Lins, the idol of the masses, received a remarkable ovation.

Night of 11/12 March: I fell asleep at my desk whilst waiting to jump out of the window if a revolt had broken out as planned. The sun streamed in and I awoke to find that it was all a dream. I learnt later that most of the conspirators are in jail.

26th March: Dr João Dantas, the director of the Brazilian *Diário de Notícias*, has arrived and is eager to have my case settled.

10th April: João Dantas has returned from Brazil and drawn attention to my case.

16th April: Ambassador Mendes Viana has arrived. He has described in highly coloured terms what an enthusiastic welcome I would receive in Rio, but I remained firm and repeated my conditions: the necessary papers must be handed over inside the Embassy and a member of the diplomatic corps must accompany me to the airport.

20th April: Ambassador Viana called me to see him and I found myself in a room full of people. He proposed unacceptable conditions and said that the papers must be handed over at the airport. I replied that in that case I would stay. I left but was called back shortly afterwards. João Dantas had been on the phone to Teotónio Pereira who had been ordered to speed up this case. They know better than I how they eventually reached an agreement. I only know that I handed in my papers at the Embassy and was accompanied to the airport by the first Secretary, Alarico de Oliveira.

21st April: My feet touched Brazilian soil and I arrived in my second homeland. It was the anniversary of Tiradentes.

PART FOUR

CHAPTER XV

Life in exile

I ARRIVED in Rio de Janeiro on Tiradentes' Day, 21st April 1959, and received an enthusiastic welcome, in spite of the short notice of my arrival. The first few minutes were full of greetings, emotion and the Latin embraces the effusiveness of which is so often far in excess of their sincerity. I noticed that by the time I reached the hotel several letters had already accumulated in my pockets, written by fellow members of the Opposition who criticized their colleagues and offered their services as my 'councillors'.

After living for eight years among Anglo-Saxons as well as making some fifty journeys all over the world, I was surprised at the sensational character of certain newspapers. *Manchete*, for example, managed to get a reporter into my apartment in the Hotel Glória, who not only caused me great inconvenience and made misleading statements about me but, when he discovered that I was jotting down the first pages of a novel called *Elsa*, actually decided to splash his story across the front page with the headline: 'There is a woman in Delgado's Life.' No woman was mentioned in the article, but this was enough to catch the eye on a newstand.

Television was even worse and two reporters from the same company vied with each other to secure an interview with me, although they pretended they were working together. Becoming suspicious, I declared that in order to avoid unpleasantness I would appear with both of them, and I still have a copy of the agreement which proves this. When this was ready for signature, one of them failed to turn up and, although there was nothing in the contract regarding payment, the other surreptitiously handed me 20,000 cruzeiroes. As the President of the 'General Humberto Delgado Association', Dr Luis Carvalhal, and the Treasurer, Sr Hovacio da Silva Ribeiro, were also present in my apartment, I asked the latter to sign a receipt for this money and send it to the Association which has educational and charitable aims. The reporter accepted the agreement and then suddenly asked me if I would mind adding my own signature. Naïvely, I did so, only to find that the reporter who had absented himself from the signing most unethically launched a disgraceful campaign against me, claiming that I had accepted the money for the interview. The reason for this has never been fully explained to me: I did not keep the money and, even if I had, there was nothing wrong with that, for the crew of the *Santa Maria* were paid for their interviews and, I believe, Sr Carlos Prestes was too, while in fact, I received nothing. Some of my friends thought the campaign was started because I had 'received' too little and others because it was too much. Humanity is indeed absurd and this was one of the times in my new life as an exile from my country and profession when I felt the greatest loathing for *homo sapiens*. I had never imagined that reporters could behave in such a disgusting manner.

Anti-Salazarist organizations

A charitable and educational association was formed in Rio de Janeiro, as I have already said, using my name and with myself as patron. The President, Luiz Carvalhal, had lost his teacher's diploma for taking part in Norton de Matos's electoral campaign. Afterwards, he had not been allowed to earn his living in any other profession. As soon as I arrived in Brazil I was aware that many of my fellow members of the Opposition disapproved of this move. Now the association has branches in São Paulo with Joaquim Carvalhal as President, and in Belo Horizonte under Virgolino Pereira Vilhena and although it is not a political organization, it does counter-balance the 'Dr Oliveira Salazar Association', and a large part of the working-class belongs to it. In São Paulo there existed, and still does exist, the old Portuguese

Republican Centre founded in 1908. These two were the only legally constituted organizations I found when I arrived and both were in difficulties. A small group existed, without official recognition, who issued protests to the press and occasionally accomplished something worthwhile. It had the vague title of 'The Committee of Intellectuals'.

Another necessarily unofficial organization was the National Independent Movement, founded on 18th June 1958, of which I am the leader. This was organized on democratic lines with a Council and Executive Committee presided over by the University Professor, Dr João Rodrigues. We used this association as a means of contact with all those who have to live a life of bitter secrecy in Portugal.

I am not surprised that the Opposition lacks coherence, since it has never had close links with the masses and is confronted by the financial strength of the Salazarists who have State funds at their disposal, which they use for direct and indirect subsidies. There is also the fatal but undeniable fact that the overseas settlers of any nation living under a dictatorship always cling to the dictator until he dies: the German and Italian colonies in Brazil are good examples of this. Furthermore, it must be remembered that, large though it is, the Portuguese colony, unlike the Spanish, consists almost entirely of emigrants rather than exiles. After Franco's victory nearly half a million Spanish political refugees fled across the Pyrenees, and in such matters numbers are important. The Spanish colony of São Paulo, although it has fewer inhabitants than the Portuguese colony, has eight Opposition centres as opposed to two for the Portuguese.

The attempt to bring Henrique Galvão to Brazil

On 13th May 1959, while I was on an official visit to São Paulo, Galvão passed through Rio on his way to Argentina. Excited and pleased with this new setback for the dictator, we talked together over the phone, Later, however, none of my efforts to obtain a visa for him had any success. Both of us had taken part in the 28th May revolt and moreover had developed a close friendship for each other over the years, and so naturally the dictator did not want us to get together.

Now that my military career was ruined I began to look for work and, although there was some opportunity in Rio, Salazarist pressure made it difficult for me to obtain any means of livelihood. My colleagues in the Opposition were unable to help, and while I was in this miserable situation, Princess Maria Pia of Saxe-Coburg, the legitimate daughter of King Carlos I, invited me to go to Italy with her family, but I refused this generous offer.

Finally, in January 1960, a Brazilian, Rui Amaral Lemos, the founder of the Cestas de Natal firm, offered me a post as Director of Public Relations in his 'Amaral Selected Foods' factory.

Brazilian youth

I should like to say a word about the young people in Brazil for, besides the many newspapers who showed their appreciation of our problems, the students offered us valuable help, based on their natural vitality and youthful enthusiasm. It was a surprise to discover what power they had, and when Brazil has passed through her present turbulent phase they will surely have something valuable to contribute to their country's future.

I shall never forget how, when my children, aged twelve, were at school in the U.S.A., they voted to select those of their fellows most suited for certain tasks. In the Army School at West Point I watched cadets discussing the colour question under a jury of colonels, as part of their training for parliamentary-type debating.

The outrageous affair of the banquet given for Negrão de Lima

This was announced as being a public event and therefore my colleagues suggested that I should apply for admission, which was a perfectly reasonable proposal since Negrão de Lima was the Minister for Foreign Affairs during my time in asylum and he was now going to Lisbon as Ambassador.

The banquet was, however, almost entirely a Salazarist affair and people started to advise and threaten me about it, which only made me more determined to go. I engaged a lawyer, Dr João Gonçalves Neto, who contacted the Brazilian judicial authority and obtained official confirmation that I had a right to attend the banquet.

At the stated time I appeared at the door, although I saw it was barred by supporters of the régime. A hand shot out to stop me and I retaliated by pushing it away in what a newspaper described as a 'tiger-like' manner. The police intervened, not to help me enter, but to advise me to leave. I stood firm and stuck to my conditions even when President Kubitschek sent a message through the Ambassador, Alcenar, requesting me to leave. I said that I would not go away until the Brazilian judge revoked his statement and declared that both he and I had misunderstood the Constitution of Brazil. At 11.30 he did so and I went away.

O Diário de Notícias said in an article by Osorio Borba, published on 20th November 1959, two days after the banquet: 'This was all we needed: here in Brazil, in our own capital city, Salazarism is applying its totalitarian and forcible National Union methods and with shameful disrespect for a decision of Brazilian justice. It was correct and natural for General Humberto Delgado to want to participate in this act of respect to the ex-Minister of Brazilian Foreign Affairs, who had approved and supported the action of ex-Ambassador Álvaro Lins when he granted political asylum to the leader of the Portuguese Opposition and guaranteed him a safe journey to Brazil.

'. . . General Humberto Delgado was treated in a brutal manner at the door of the Gymnasium, but he retaliated with true courage. . . . Finally, Judge Parim, or Paim or Paraim, as he is variously called, did himself a bad turn by publicly cancelling, under Luso-Brazilian police pressure, the mandate that he had issued guaranteeing General Humberto Delgado and his friends a safe entry to the reception.

'Is it possible that the evolution of history has been reversed and we are once more in the age of Dona Maria I and Tiradentes?'

The next day I left for England, and at the airport I was confronted by a whole battery of photographers and reporters, who wanted to see what effect the scuffle had had upon me. But they were disappointed, for I was unmarked; the blood that had been seen at the door of the Gymnasium was not mine, but came from someone else's head which I had grazed with a ring on my finger.

This incident proves two things: firstly, the depths to which the country has sunk under the dictatorship, for such things being able to happen to a general, and one well versed in war and politics at that. Secondly, the depths to which the Opposition had sunk, for some of its members felt an effeminate horror when I countered violence with violence.

Visits Abroad

In contrast to the Northern races the Latins are full of ideas but incapable of putting them into effect; they always consider people before principles. It is not surprising therefore that with their tendency to talk rather than act they have usually been left behind in international competition. This thought came to me when I was on a visit to Venezuela which, mingled with several amusing incidents, did prove one thing to me. It all began when I was instructed to arrive on a certain Saturday, only to find that my Portuguese friends had not realized that there was no flight from Brazil that day. So I had to put my journey forward twenty-four hours, take a plane to Trinidad, stay the night there and the next day catch the local plane which flies between the island and Caracas. Because my money was not due to arrive until the eve of my journey, I had to borrow some for my fare, which was not paid back to my hosts until some months later.

These small incidents are not being recounted for amusement but because they each form a piece in the colourful mosaic which is the Portuguese Opposition, with all its verbiage, absent-mindedness and lack of efficiency. However, Latin enthusiasm has its good points and the journey was eventually brought to a successful conclusion and I am extremely grateful to those colleagues of mine in the Opposition who sponsored the trip.

Venezuela is a pleasant country, happy, enthusiastic and full of faith in the future, although perhaps rather too South American for someone who, like myself, has an orderly mind and has lived for so many years among Anglo-Saxons. I adapted myself as best I could to the unbelievable lack of efficiency which once meant that I had to be fetched to a newspaper office at 6.30 p.m. for an interview scheduled to take place at 3 p.m., but without my being informed of it. The gay '*no se preocupe*' ('not to worry)' attitude, which one constantly encounters under the blue Venezuelan sky, was difficult to accept especially when I was extremely worried, such as on the occasion when there were not enough funds to pay my fare home. Yet, in spite of all its characteristics which can so easily disconcert a European, this is a great country.

As to the Portuguese Opposition in Venezuela, I received the usual impression that it was composed of a few dozen active members with no *esprit de corps*, and these were united in little groups of sometimes less than ten, which felt an intense hatred for each other. This is in accordance with the rule, paradoxical but true, of Gustave the Good, who declared that the greatest enmity exists between similar elements rather than between those whose ideas are totally different.

England

After a few days in Rio, I set off for England on 19th November 1959, breaking my journey in Caracas for a few moments to confer with Henrique Galvão, Costa Mota, Cezarino Calafete and Mário Mendes. I travelled via New York and Prestwick to Amsterdam, whence I turned back for London, the friends who had arranged the trip not having realized that Prestwick was in Britain. Thus my going on to Holland was unnecessary; within a few days, moreover, I was due to return there on the next stage of my journey.

On the 22nd, I arrived in London and was received by members of the three parties. My reception exceeded anything I had expected and so did the welcome by the press.

The day I arrived I had the pleasure of dining with my old friend, Ivor Bulmer-Thomas, whom I had known since 1945, when I was first appointed Director-General of Civil Aviation. He was Under-Secretary of Aviation at that time, which meant that we had worked together on the aviation agreement between Britain and Portugal.

The next day, to my great joy, my wife arrived. Since I

am so restless she, poor woman, leads a very agitated life when after twenty-five years of marriage she should be enjoying some rest and recompense for the wonderful qualities she has shown as a wife and mother.

The programme for my stay in London was somewhat rigorous, for it had been organized by the Portuguese with the best intentions, but it was unpractical and gave me no time for quiet reflection—or even a second shave. At times I had to be firm with my Portuguese friends who had had little experience in these affairs. The most annoying part was that we were occasionally late for appointments, but generally speaking the Portuguese Committee, in conjunction with the British delegates, made a good, worthwhile job of the arrangements.

Apart from the Portuguese, whose names had better be kept secret, I was received by the Secretary of the International Department of the Labour Party, Mr David Ennals, by a delegation of Liberal members, including Mr Harold Glanville, the Vice-President of the National Liberal Club, and by several other people. The visit aroused widespread interest, beginning at the airport, where a battery of television and newspaper reporters was waiting for me, an exceptional situation for the Portuguese Opposition.

It is true that my visit had been arranged by the Labour Party, but it was an even greater slap in the face for the dictator for me to be hospitably received by the other two parties. Britain is the truest democracy in the world and our oldest ally, closely linked with Portugal in the geographical, political and economic spheres.

Yet I must emphasize that this is also one of the countries where the legend of Salazar's 'paternalism' has been most carefully fostered, thanks to the extravagant propaganda (at the expense of the Portuguese people) extolling the virtues of the dictator and his Government, which is directed particularly to Britain and to the United States. Another reason for this legend's success in Britain is that the dictator was finally compelled to concede air bases in the Azores to the Allies during the Second World War. The British press referred to me as 'The Azores Man' and this aroused the public's curiosity more than ever.

My visit turned out to be an overwhelming success for the Portuguese Opposition, more so indeed than even the most optimistic of them had dared to expect. I had been to Britain often on official duties and was well aware that the people's gratitude and courtesy would never allow them to forget an old friend who had helped them negotiate the Azores concession, but even so, I must confess that I had not expected such a welcome.

A large number of organizations showed some sort of acknowledgement of the situation in Portugal, for example, the Royal Institute of International Affairs, the National Peace Council, the Fabian Society, the British-Asian and Overseas Socialist Fellowship, and the National Liberal Club. Unfortunately, for health reasons, and because of a particularly heavy programme, I had to cancel many invitations. I wrote articles in the *New Statesman*, the *London Quarterly* and the *Contemporary Review*.

Just consider the difference between all this and the Portuguese *Diário de Manhã*, which all the Portuguese pay for but do not read. This paper compared my visit to England with a tub-thumping session in Hyde Park!

The subjects which aroused most interest in the British press were the disgraceful way in which Portugal's totalitarian state was run, its famine economy, the objects of my visit to England and the methods envisaged for ousting Salazar.

The *Evening Standard* said on 21st November: 'We have reason to be grateful to Delgado. During the black days of 1940, when the Portuguese Government was cheerfully contemplating a Nazi victory in Europe, he made himself highly unpopular by arguing that Britain should be given air bases in the Azores. It was only in 1943, when it became obvious that Portugal had put its money on the wrong horse, that the Government agreed to the plan. We rewarded Delgado with a C.B.E.' On the 26th, Paul Johnson wrote in the same paper in exactly the same vein.

Holland

When I arrived in Amsterdam, the police corps which deals with foreigners told me that the Minister of Justice had decided that I was not to make any public statements, not even to the press. It seems that he was under pressure from the Government in Lisbon who were once more trying to trap me by circulating the rumour that I was a Communist or working with the Communists and therefore a dangerous element. However, later, after considerable criticism in the press of the Minister of Justice's action, this decision was revoked and I held a press conference which was also televised.

When I heard of the Minister of Justice's first decision, I decided to leave Holland as soon as possible and return to Brazil, since firstly it did not seem sensible to stay where I was *persona non grata*, and secondly it would have been practically impossible at this late date to alter the schedule of my visits to the other countries. I was even more determined to leave when the Belgian Minister in Holland informed me that I should be subject to the same restrictions if I went to Belgium. This decision was also revoked the next day when a member of the Belgian Diplomatic Corps told me that I could go to his country and speak freely in public. I thanked him but replied that it was too late now and I would avoid even flying over Belgium. I am sure that Salazar must have hinted at colonial problems in his telegrams to these two countries.

The terrible expense of the telegrams I had to send on account of these troubles and the indisposition from which I had suffered on arrival from England, in fact, everything, urged me to cancel the rest of the itinerary: France, Germany and Sweden. I did so, but on account of some technical difficulties in transmission I believe that some countries did not receive my telegram in time: I am 'Not Guilty', but I am sorry.

CHAPTER XVI

The *Santa Maria* affair

AFTER countless visits to the Itamarati,[1] with the object of an entry visa for Henrique Galvão, I was finally given a straightforward answer on 18th November 1959 and refused a visa.

Veiled threats about having me sent out of the country made me realize that I should have to take the greatest care how I behaved in Brazil—at least until Kubitschek's Government had fallen.

For more than a quarter of a century the presence of Salazar's police and the general weariness induced by the antics of previous politicians had combined to subdue the spirit of armed rebellion in Portugal. The politically inclined officers of the Army of the First Republic were now in their seventies, whilst others had always been considered as anti-Army rebels, even before Salazar came to power.

A good number of these are abroad, some now rich, and others still toiling laboriously for a living, but the great majority of the officers on the active list have never heard of the old revolutionaries. However, I must emphasize that there are no more than half a dozen of them in Brazil.

Undoubtedly, it was when I began to make contacts in Portugal on my return to Europe from Washington that the idea of armed revolt as a practical proposition was revived and later, when I left my post and was appointed Director-General of Civil Aviation for the second time, I began to

[1] The Brazilian Foreign Office is known as the Itamarati after the palace in Rio. (Translator)

instigate a revolt, even though I had no military command.

I have already described in an earlier chapter the three revolutions which were planned down to the last detail in the two years following the first in June 1958, when the officers unexpectedly withdrew at the last moment. In the next, planned for 12th March 1959, the men were already at their posts, when two of the officers panicked as soon as they encountered the commander of one of the units they were supposed to take over. When the revolt was discovered by P.I.D.E., those who had taken part were court-martialled and the hearing dragged on until the July of the following year. I did not think that our supporters could be reorganized and a new revolt planned in less than six months, so perhaps in the summer of 1961. . . .

At the beginning of 1959 Manuel Serra, and some half a dozen others who had been involved in the revolt on 12th March, reached Brazil. Major Calafate, who had sought asylum in the Venezuelan Embassy and then gone into exile in Venezuela, also joined us later, but he had had a serious quarrel with Henrique Galvão and consequently withdrew from politics. Obviously, before the middle of 1961, the time was not ripe for a revolution either in Portugal or in Brazil.

The Communist Party proved an additional obstacle, as did the oldest Opposition newspaper in Brazil, *Portugal Democrático*, who objected to any plan to overthrow the dictatorship by violent means. They would prefer to do so by elections, but they did not explain how they expected to do this through such elections as the Portuguese Government allows.

The revolutionary spirit was only re-awoken a short while before my electoral campaign and then only among the younger members of the Army, a most important point. Yet, because of the failure of the last attempt to revolt, these feelings subsided. Men began to make plans again but only in the strictest secrecy, for the Kubitschek government was unwilling to accept the Portuguese Opposition.

Two months before the Lisbon trials of those involved in the 12th March revolt ended, Henrique Galvão told me of his plan to capture the *Santa Maria*. I was on a propaganda mission to Venezuela and we met there, for the Venezuelan

Government's attitude to the Portuguese and Spanish opposi-
tions is exactly the opposite to Kubitschek's in Brazil.

On 12th April 1960, he wrote me a letter describing his
plan which was that a hundred Portuguese and Spaniards
should board and take possession of the *Santa Maria* on the
high seas. With typical Latin optimism, they expected 20%
of the crew and the captain himself who, they presumed,
would not be Salazarist, to support them. They would then
sail to the Spanish island of Fernando Pó in the Gulf of Guinea
and the Portuguese would subsequently attack São Tomé,
the Portuguese island nearby, and the north of Angola. Afterwards they hoped to be able to obtain asylum in Ghana. I
was to join them at the end of this first phase.

This was all to be under the aegis of the famous D.R.I.L.
(Iberian Revolutionary Directory for Liberation) which
today would better be termed the Spanish Revolutionary
Directory for Liberation, since Portuguese are no longer
included. Only much later, after the *Santa Maria* had arrived
in Brazil, was I able to discover that none of the Portuguese,
not even Galvão himself, knew exactly what D.R.I.L. was;
his knowledge of it was confined to its rather dramatic title
and the isolated terrorist activities which it had promoted in
Spain. It certainly did not live up to the claims of its leaders
who, when they arrived in Recife, said that they had 2,500
suicide commandoes. They overdid it there, even if one makes
allowances for Iberian 'elaboration'.

There was some question as to whether I should take part
in the first phase of the operation, assuming of course that the
Brazilian Government would allow me to leave the country,
for my passport was in the hands of the authorities, pending
the delivery of a pass-book No. 19, which is a residence permit
for foreigners. I was eventually given this at the end of
1960.

After discussion we agreed unanimously that I would not
take part in the first phase because we would be running the
risk of losing both leaders at the same time.

Entanglement with the Spaniards

I immediately told them of my doubts regarding their plan.

Although I am in favour of co-operation with the Spaniards and in fact have signed an agreement with their government, there is great difference between carrying out combined operations with the troops of two countries and mixing Portuguese and Spaniards together in small combat units, especially if they are both used against the same objective. The Portuguese, belonging to the smaller nation of the two, and accustomed to looking upon the Castilians as their traditional enemy, would straightway feel inferior, just as the average Portuguese does today, in spite of the arguments put forward by intellectuals.

After I had put my point of view to Galvão and heard his opinion, I finally agreed, for the nature of the operation seemed to make co-operation necessary, and also the first port of call was a Spanish island. As he was worried about the small proportion of Portuguese taking part, he asked me to find fifteen or twenty men from Brazil whose fares would be paid from funds in Venezuela. I mentioned the plan to two officers in São Paulo, who were old political émigrés, only to receive emphatic advice not to think of such a thing.

Fortunately in Rio, where people are always inclined to act rather than theorize, twenty-three men immediately volunteered.

In case the reader thinks that I was abusing my rights as a political exile, I must point out that the operation would not begin from Brazil. Anyway, the capture of the ship which should have taken place in June or July was postponed five or six times for various reasons of which the most important was lack of money. The volunteers I had found in Brazil backed out one by one until I was left with two or three radio and navigation technicians. We started to collect subscriptions in order to obtain the necessary funds, but one day they had the idea in Venezuela of taking a Spanish ship which would stop at the Canary Isles. However, when this burst of optimism had passed, they not only failed to pay the passages of the Portuguese to Venezuela, but Galvão also asked that these men should be given their fares to Spain. As Captain Pimental, who was over seventy, explained, some members of the Portuguese Opposition in Brazil were afraid that they would be faced with another 'Queirogada'.[1] Apart from this, when collections were made at a dinner on 5th October, it was only too clear that there were going to be some petty squabbles over funds.

In September 1960 Galvão asked me for a reference, as he had done once before when he wanted to be given a command in the Iberian Directory. Here is the more important of the two I gave him:

'As National Independent candidate for the Presidency of the Republic, who represented the Opposition in the elections of 8th June 1958, during which the Portuguese Government issued an official statement forbidding the supervision of the elections by Opposition agents:

—Also, as Leader of the National Independent Movement, founded on 18th June 1958 to represent the Portuguese Opposition, and

—In view of the delay of the Brazilian authorities in granting me a permit for permanent residence, and their having held my passport for several months;

—but taking into account the fact that, if these circumstances restrict what I can do towards the liberation of Portugal, they cannot prevent me from delegating powers:

'I DECLARE that I appoint as my plenipotentiary delegate in all actions mentioned below, Sr Henrique Galvão, a former officer in the Army and former colonial chief inspector, whom I have nominated as General Secretary of the National Independent Movement and to whom I delegate

THE FOLLOWING POWERS:

a) To create and employ any means necessary for the liberation of our Homeland, representing me on land, on sea and in the air in my legitimate capacity as supreme authority of the Portuguese Nation, according to the belief and asseveration of the Opposition, based upon trustworthy proofs of fraud in the elections;

b) As soon as the plenipotentiary delegate reaches

---

[1] Queiroga was an officer who had set out from Brazil to start a revolt and had returned without accomplishing his object.

Portuguese soil, or its equivalent, including ship or plane, and considers the time opportune to establish a National Independent Junta of Liberation (J.N.I.L.) which, with the help of other local dependent organizations, shall proceed with the operations of liberation, occupation, administration and the maintenance of public order, in the spirit of the National Independent candidature and of the National Independent Movement which followed it.

1. The plenipotentiary delegate, and/or the afore-mentioned organizations, shall keep me constantly informed regarding the preparations and operations for the liberation and occupation in order that I may make the necessary arrangements.

2. According to circumstances, I beg, advise and command all authorities to give the plenipotentiary delegate, either directly or indirectly, the greatest moral and material assistance with the aim of liberating the Portuguese Nation from the slavery of the totalitarian government.

'For our Homeland and for Liberty!'

On 8th October, before the departure was postponed for the second time, I sent a coded alert signal to Rio so that the Portuguese there would be ready to embark at Curaçao on 11th or 12th October. However, as I received no news from Venezuela, I presumed that the operation had been postponed until the 30th. There were, I believe, two more postponements, the first until the middle of November and the second to January 1961. Unfortunately, we were confronted by a very serious problem, for those involved had given up their jobs long before they were able to leave Brazil. Not only was no money coming through from Venezuela, but we had to give them financial help. I started a collection and sent them a small sum of money of something like 50,000 cruzeiros, which at that time was worth about 300 dollars. Admittedly this was only a small sum, but it helped to relieve their state of poverty, wellnigh of destitution, in fact, and moreover it turned out to be, so Galvão informed me, almost equal to the total contributions from Portugal, France, Canada and the United States.

A Loan

Meanwhile I was in Brazil, making my preparations in case nothing came of this operation or if it did not even reach the discussion stage. On 27th September 1960, I went to see a Brazilian capitalist who had offered to give financial backing to our struggle, but he told me that he could not do so before February or March 1961, since the construction of the Via Anchieta was draining away all the money at his disposal —nearly a hundred million! Finally we agreed on 29th May as the date for me to receive the loan of 3,350,000 cruzeiros, which was to be for the plan known as 'I/K'. However, he suddenly changed his mind and nearly gave me a heart attack by telling me this only four days before the loan was due. There were many other similar incidents but it is not worth giving details of such a sorry story, which is in fact so depressing that it needs a very strong will to keep one's spirits up.

Galvão's Declaration of Loyalty

On 30th September 1960, Galvão sent me the following declaration:

'I, Henrique Carlos Malta Galvão, who have been appointed by General Humberto Delgado as Secretary-General of the National Independent Movement and special delegate of that Movement in Venezuela, declare on my honour that, since General Humberto Delgado has entrusted me with the task of preparing and leading the struggle for national liberation called DULCINEA within the framework of the Iberian Revolutionary Directory of Liberation, I shall do my utmost faithfully to carry out this mission as far as my powers and opportunities permit and with the co-operation of the devoted companions who accompany me, according to the instructions received.

'I should naturally like to add that I recognize General

Humberto Delgado as the only legitimate and effective leader of the Portuguese Democratic Opposition, for he has been designated as such by the Portuguese people.

'I confirm this document with my signature and finger-prints.

'Caracas, 30th September 1960.

'Henrique Galvão.'

New hope

On Christmas Day 1960 Henrique Galvão told me that he would let me know between 10th and 12th January whether or not the operation was going to be put into effect; if it was, it was going to be carried out during the last ten days of January. I had already explained to him that if the operation had to be cancelled we would both suffer the consequences for, although we had planned it in the strictest secrecy, a large number of people were involved. Galvão also suggested that he should come to Brazil on the *Santa Maria* in order to seek asylum there, which undoubtedly would cause quite a sensation and he asked me how I thought they would be received.

On 1st January 1961, I made an urgent appeal for enough money to enable him to leave Venezuela, for if the operation was not carried out, I knew that he would not be able to stay on in Venezuela, where feelings were already running high and the cancellation of the plan could easily bring them to a head. On 18th January, he told me that he had heard that Franco had sent a warship to Fernando Pó as a result of the attacks made upon him in the United Nations. Galvão came to the conclusion that we now had two possibilities open to us:

1) If Franco had indeed sent the warship, the operation against São Tomé and Angola would be impossible.

2) If he had not, we could stick to the original plan.

If the rumour was true, he thought the best idea was to make a series of raids upon São Tomé and Angola and then, since it was impossible to continue with the rest of the plan, they would be 'forced to seek asylum in Brazil'.

I found all this talk about morale-raising raids and a return journey across the Atlantic somewhat confusing, but it was too late to write to him about it. The important Spanish agents who were to come and see me cancelled their visit.

The start of the voyage

Three days later, on 21st January, Galvão sent me the following telegram from Curaçao:

'We leave in two hours. Long letter following.'

I anxiously began to study the newspapers. We know now that when the boat was taken over, a member of the crew was seriously wounded and through kind-heartedness or for some reason unknown, those in command of the *Santa Maria* decided to put him ashore on the island of Santa Lucia. (Apart from this one casualty, one officer of the crew was killed.) This meant that the ship not only gave away its position, but also let it be known that there was a rebellion on board, and this while she was still a long way from the African coast— in fact, she had hardly left South American waters.

On 24th January the papers published the telegram from Ottawa, dated on the 23rd, stating that there were rebels, or rather pirates, aboard the *Santa Maria*. Immediately I read this I sent the following telegram at 9.30 a.m. to the British and American Embassies in Rio:

'Request Your Excellency to inform your Government immediately that the *Santa Maria* incident is not mutiny or piracy, but appropriation of a Portuguese vessel by Portuguese people for Portuguese political purposes. I earnestly beg your Government not to interfere in this matter.'

At 2.30 p.m. I received the following telegram from Galvão:

'The mission accomplished successfully after very short fight for possession. All our men acted with commendable calmness and courage. I confirm simultaneous communication made to the press which from all over world is eagerly seeking information. Naturally, insults and calumny from Salazar's papers. The crew accepts the situation and obeys orders. The majority of the passengers support us whole-heartedly. Absolute calmness and security on board and life is perfectly normal. All are well and ask for greetings to be sent to their families. Please consult specialists in international law and obtain due recognition of the act of insurrection and consequent state of hostilities. We are following our secret course and send greetings to Your Excellency who, by the will of the Portuguese people, is Head of State. I shall send further communications whenever possible without divulging our secret destination and operational plans. We will never surrender. Please inform our families and the Portuguese people, whom Your Excellency represents, that we are well and send our greetings. In accordance with the authority conferred upon me by Your Excellency, the National Independent Junta of Liberation has been created as a political, military and administrative organ of the National Independent Movement. We shall disembark passengers at the first neutral port which will allow us to do so without interning the ship. We especially wish to do this on account of the sympathy and understanding shown to us by all, including the foreigners. Greetings to the people, the press and the President-elect of Brazil, to whom we express our deep gratitude for his support of our Cause. For our Homeland and for Liberty.'

I replied:

'Re message of 24th, wish to inform you of profound enthusiasm of Portuguese and Brazilians. Greetings to our great leader, Henrique Galvão, and his brave companions who are worthy of their motto, "Honour or death". For the Homeland and for Liberty.'

Costa Mora of Venezuela suggested in a telegram that I should send the men a signal 'like Nelson's at Trafalgar'.

The press

The press soon began to invade my house and turn it into

194

chaos and I was kept busy answering the telephone. I received telegrams asking for information from South America, the United States, Canada, Europe and even from Africa. There was little time for thought or relaxation. I immediately told the whole world that I claimed full responsibility for the action; this was done quite frankly, not, as certain malicious people have suggested, in order to win the laurels which rightfully belonged to someone else and of which moreover I have no need. In order to prove this, I sent the *Daily Mail* in London a telegram saying that we had started to make plans in April 1960, following a suggestion made to me by Galvão.

The *Diário de Notícias* in Rio took an objective view of the whole affair in an article 'O Momento International'. They emphasized that it was perfectly reasonable for me to take full responsibility.

On the 26th, I sent a telegram to President Kennedy:

'As an exiled colleague, former representative in N.A.T.O., former military and air attaché in Washington and an old friend of the United States, I request that the American Navy should discontinue their surveillance of the *Santa Maria* since this is destroying the necessary secrecy of the ship's movements. Respectfully.'

The same day I presented my compliments to the French through *France Soir* and the next day through *Paris Match*.

On the 27th, assuming that the *Santa Maria* was sailing for Africa, I told Galvão:

'The experts consider it doubtful whether Jânio Quadros will take power on the 31st. Ascension Island seems a good idea and I have sent a telegram to this effect to the leader of the Labour Party. I like the high seas idea; the transfer would thus take four hours. Otherwise pass responsibility to the Americans. Warmest regards. Humberto.' I was advising him to continue eastwards.

As I expected, the press soon turned against me, forgetting my statements to them, and they even behaved so childishly and spitefully as to publish such an important document as the credentials I had given to Galvão on 23rd September

1960; they included this in the small items and claimed that I had sent it to Galvão only a few days before. Some would settle these small matters differently, by knuckling under to self-important young men, but honesty pays in the long run, even though some fools claim that this proved my lack of capacity for political manoeuvre.

Whether the ship was to go East or West

Since the ship seemed to be setting her course towards Brazil, I sent a telegram to President Jânio Quadros on the 29th:

'The last telegram I received from Galvão told me that he intended to sail to a port in the north of Brazil, and this must have crossed mine in which I suggested other means of disembarking the passengers. However, I think he will probably make for a Brazilian port, but the final decision lies with him. On the assumption that Your Excellency has already taken office, he has asked me to seek Your Excellency's support. I should like to thank you for the lucid and friendly statements you have made to the press, and renew my urgent request to be allowed to see Your Excellency. For the Homeland and for Liberty.'

The same day I sent a long and expensive telegram to Galvão outlining my ideas and also those of Álvaro Lins, who gave information concerning the statements of the President, Jânio Quadros. In this telegram I insisted once more upon the advantages of disembarking the passengers at sea or on Ascension Island, without of course ignoring his suggestion that the ship should sail to a Brazilian port, I recommended him to remain in international waters until noon on the 31st, when Quadros was due to take office.

Meanwhile I, being obliged to stay on land, was loyally repeating that we would never surrender and that, if necessary, we would scuttle the ship.

Unfortunately the Santa Maria *sails to Brazil*

Our fate was already sealed, for the ship berthed in Brazil

General Delgado photographed during a news conference at
London airport, November 1959

The *Santa Maria* moving into Recife Harbour on the morning of 2nd February 1961

and the guerrilla tactics began. The quaint incident of the *Tribuna da Imprensa*, comes into the picture here. On the 24th, it screamed out the headline: 'Pirates have taken possession of the *Santa Maria*'. On the 25th: 'This must not be allowed. Plain piracy is serious enough, but in this case one man has been killed and several others injured.' The next day it continued in the same vein.

Meanwhile some hysterical woman claimed to possess some twenty letters from Galvão and hinted that she had been the inspiration of the *Santa Maria* affair and heaven knows what else besides.

A telegram requesting information suddenly appeared on board the ship from 'Calacerda', the telegraphic address of the newspaper, but Galvão thought that it came from Carlos Lacerda, the Minister for Foreign Affairs. Therefore, if he had refused to reply, he would have been withholding information from the press while, if he did reply, as in fact he did, Carlos Lacerda would have had grounds for interfering.

The paper abruptly turned a somersault for, after attacking Galvão and myself, even to the extent of advising the Itamarati to suppress my political activities, it began to support Galvão, while treating me like some poor idiot who did not know what he was doing.

This happened on the 30th when Lacerda was acting as a sort of Deputy President of the Republic. When I saw that Galvão was falling into the trap, I sent him a telegram pointing out that if he carried on like this, it would be as if the boat were asking permission from the Civil Governor of Lisbon to enter the Tagus. As for Ambassador Álvaro Lins, the *Tribuna da Imprensa* refused to acknowledge his existence.

In Recife

On the 29th I went to Rio and then two days later to Recife where I held a press conference. Everyone wanted to know if, after so many expressions of enthusiasm both on board the ship and on land, she was going to continue on her course, be sunk or surrender. As far as I was concerned, the enterprise was finished, since, although I had insisted that they sailed eastward, they were heading for Brazil.

On the night of 1/2nd February, I managed to get on board the *Santa Maria* by means of a fishing boat hired by Messrs Miller, Snalle and Rickerby, reporters from *Life* and *Time*. This was not an easy task, for two destroyers, one American and one Brazilian, were blockading the ship and also the cost of hiring the boat was extremely high on account of the risk involved. Consequently we had to sail without lights.

Galvão and I talked together in private for a few moments until the 'officers' arrived. This was in the middle of the night, but we were photographed and spoke to the journalists who had come with me. I realized how stupid it would be for the ship to continue, since both money and crew would be difficult to find.

On the 2nd, Admiral Dias Fernandes, the naval Commander in that area, came to see me and asked me to ensure that there were no complications, for Galvão had suggested that with Lins and myself he should go to Brasilia for discussions with President Quadros, but I did not agree. That night I went to see the Admiral, but he told me it was too late to go aboard. However he promised I should the next day. As negotiations for the surrender of the ship were to take place later in the day, I told them that in my opinion it was not advisable to pursue a project which, however fascinating, was finished with, and it would be unwise to complicate matters. As I was never given an official account of the outcome, I shall make no further comments. On the 4th I set out for Rio.

On 30th April I gave written confirmation that the National Independent Movement was not represented on the Iberian Revolutionary Directory for Liberation. I was therefore rather amused by the people who declared in July 1961 that either I had never belonged to the *soi disant* organization or that I had been expelled from it!

The Luso-Spanish Agreement

This had been drawn up by D. Felix Gordon Ordza and myself and was eventually concluded and signed on 26th November 1960 by the Air Force General, D. Emílio Herrera, Prime Minister of the Spanish Government in exile. It was kept secret until the change of régime in Brazil. As the *Santa*

Maria affair occurred at the same time, our agreement was finally made public on 10th February 1961 in São Paulo. It is a sort of gentlemen's agreement covering three phases:

1) Until the constitution of the first liberation government;
2) After the constitution of the first liberation government;
3) After the complete liberation of the two countries.

CHAPTER XVII

Angola and the colonial plan of the Opposition

PORTUGAL, lying as it does between the sea and Castile, realized after the struggle with Spain in the fifteenth century, that expansion towards the east was impossible. Therefore it became absorbed in the so-called 'maritime epic', which was to engage the greater part of the country in establishing and occupying various settlements along the newly discovered coast-lines of Africa, Asia and Oceania.

A period of serious interest in Africa began at the end of the last century. Various scientific missions set out such as those of Serpa Pinto, Capelo and Ivens, roads were constructed, as were railways and telegraph systems, and in their wake came groups of settlers such as the one in Luanda led by Henrique de Carvalho or the one under Paiva Couceiro which travelled from Bié to Mucusso up the Cubango to Andara; thus great names appeared and helped to exorcise the evil spirit of the Berlin Conference in 1885. In 1906 a native tax was authorized, which was first collected in 1908.

In the south of Angola, occupation was established during the years 1904 to 1915 and the name of Alves Roçadas is especially memorable as a fine military chief and governor. Other men in the Government also come to mind, such as Eduardo Costa (1905–7) and his successor, Paiva Couceiro (1907–9). The latter, who had been dismissed from the Army for rebelling against the republican régime, wrote the following to Dr Salazar on 30th October 1937:

'... I had always acted in the belief that the development of Angola was a national objective and that its realization depended upon close collaboration of the authorities in the metropolis, in the province itself and of private individuals. Following this theory, I considered that certain communication works on land, sea and river, economic administration and research, military defence and native education were the duties of an effective sovereignty and that, on the other hand, it was up to the farmers, industrialists, traders and settlers to decide the best use for these facilities which had been created at their own expense, and the profits from their labour and individual effort should belong to them.

'... However, instead of this, Your Excellency, who has never shown the slightest interest in our overseas activities, nor possesses the least experience in this field, has decided to impose upon Angola a certain financial system which, even in a more civilized and stable country, would not deserve the priority which Your Excellency gives it.'

Paivo Couceiro starts his letter by saying that Angola intends eventually to follow the example set by Brazil on 7th September 1822, but at the moment it has not reached a state of development to justify such a step. He adds:

'Moreover, it was Your Excellency yourself who gave rise to these ideas and to their execution' and later: 'The police and the censor are in control. Some are rendered helpless by such a repressive régime, whilst others are so intent at making what they can out of it that they have no time to pay attention to what is going on around them. Thus our country now lies in a state of collective insensibility.'

The idea of allowing the natives to choose their own work was initiated, at least in theory, by the republican doctrine, but in practice it succeeded not so much because of the decree of 13th May 1911, but on account of the strength of mind of Norton de Matos, who was governor from 1912 to 1915 and High Commissioner from 1912 to 1924. He was a shining light in the colony but certainly severely attacked and even

I criticized him when, as a young lieutenant, I used to read misleading articles in the press which showed only the worst side of his work. In fact, he represented the full flowering of the new outlook.

One of his main ideas was to transform the administration into a purely civil service, taking it out of the hands of the Army and putting it under civil control. Then he wanted to raise the status of the Negro by abolishing corporal punishment and trying to destroy the idea, which the white man had been so pleased to foster, that the native is by nature a vagrant. Working along these lines, he created native commissions which included one coloured member. He opened up roads and encouraged officials by giving them a car as soon as they had constructed 100 km. of motor roads. He developed the radio and telephone systems, established white settlements in the larger bases, founded professional schools, defined the duties of the Army, although his motives were misunderstood, and even took the first step towards installing military aviation in the colony. Exports of colonial produce increased rapidly. At the same time he checked the abuse of alcohol and imposed laws on the use and possession of weapons and gunpowder. Between 1909 and 1912, nearly 16,000 weapons and more than a million kilos of gunpowder passed through the customs!

As to the Army, Matos gave instructions to the Chief of the General Staff, which I quote from his book, *The Province of Angola* (Oporto, 1926, page 89):

'This does not mean that I do not consider military men eligible for administrative posts. On the contrary, the district governors are almost all soldiers, as are the administrators. However, they have no priority over the civilians and have been given these posts simply because, as officers, they have developed special aptitudes which are rarely found in civilians. But, while in these positions, they are no longer considered as military personnel and those officers who hold responsible posts in the administration will have to take the necessary examinations and competitive tests if they wish to continue to exercise their functions.'

Decentralization begins

The law establishing the basis for financial autonomy and colonial administrative decentralization was passed on 15th August 1914 and was followed in 1917 by the Organic Charter of the province. In 1920 the position of High Commissioner was created, with Norton de Matos as the first holder of the office, and in this post he made a special contribution in the fields of development and hygiene. At the same time an attempt was made to eliminate sleeping-sickness. He was followed by Lt.-Colonel Rego Chaves and Colonel Vicente Ferreira, who was notable for his work concerning transfers, banks, finance, credits for agriculture, production, colonization, assistance for the natives and the reform of the services, with the consequent cutting-down of expenses.

Salazar

In 1930 the Colonial Act was passed and this contains several interesting measures, such as the abolition of chartered companies, and increased protection for the native which, as Galvão proved in 1949, were never put into practice. It was also prohibited for anyone to be appointed governor who had interests in the direction or management of firms which either had head offices in the colony, or carried on any economic activity there. Any system of rule was forbidden which would compel the State to supply native labour to any economic enterprise. Then Salazar abolished the High Commissioners and curbed financial decentralization, which was easily accepted because of the chaotic state of the finances at that period. This, incidentally, had been one of the main causes of the creation of the movement which had overthrown the republican parliamentary régime.

The Colonial Act, which was integrated in the 1933 Constitution, was supplemented by the Organic Charter of the Portuguese Colonial Empire and the Administrative Reform of the Colonies, both passed in the same year, and also by the New Organization of the Colonial Ministry in 1936. It is not worth the trouble, and in fact would be almost impossible, to analyse such a wealth of documents whose intentions were so often commendable, and whose results so poor.

Nor is it any use repeating in a dry, monotonous voice, like the chirping of the cicada, the old yarn about the Negro being our brother, when slavery is still rife in São Tomé, when periods of famine still occur in the Cape Verde Islands, when forced labour is still used to enrich the white men, officials and otherwise; when the white population is leaving, and practically all the natives are still illiterate; when there is only a ridiculously small number of 'assimilated' natives, the term used for those who have become 'civilized' and therefore in theory entitled to enjoy the rights of the white man which, to judge by the plight of the 'assimilated' blacks, must be non-existent.

It was obvious to any liberal-minded person that Africa would revolt against white rule, but a reactionary such as Dr Salazar took no notice of the events of 1960 when Mauritania, Senegal, the Sudan, the Niger, the Ivory Coast, Upper Volta, Togoland, Dahomey, Nigeria, Chad, the Cameroons, Gabon, the two Congo states, the Central African Federation, Somalia and Madagascar all rebelled against white domination, as well as the countries which had been granted independence during the preceding years, such as Egypt in 1922, Libya in 1951, Morocco and French Sudan in 1956, Ghana in 1957 and Guinea in 1958.

In February 1961 the Angolan war broke out and to some extent this was the natural result of the activities of the nationalist movements which, although made up of very small minorities have great assets in the iron will of their self-appointed leaders, and in their considerable funds from abroad which are said to come either from Africans, 'reds' or Americans of a particular type.

The Opposition

For thirty-five years we have been unable to discuss any national problem and therefore it is not easy to express in a simple, accurate form the predominating ideas of the people. However, my colleagues in the Opposition badgered me so much to say something on the subject that on 5th October 1960, the fiftieth anniversary of the founding of the Republic, I announced the colonial plan of the Opposition, which I had drawn up after discussion with various people, especially Galvão, and the advisers of the National Independent Movement—both those who work in secret in Portugal and the untrammelled members in Brazil.

Apart from the small minority of abstainers, extremists and the cavilling few which one finds in every opposition, the plan was well received by our members. I sent a copy to President Kennedy, Mr Macmillan, and to Mr Hammarskjöld, the Secretary-General of the United Nations.

It was as follows:

National Independent Movement
The Colonial Plan of the Portuguese Opposition

1. The Opposition wholeheartedly disagrees with and rejects the policy of obscurantism, exploitation and violence exercised by the present totalitarian government in the colonies.

2. Although the Portuguese case is unique, on account of its four centuries of white settlement in Africa and consequent deeply rooted historic rights; and in spite of the Portuguese policy as it stands, especially with regard to miscegenation, racial harmony and social unity, the Opposition recognizes and accepts the general tendency towards the achievement at least of local autonomy for the overseas governments, believing it to be useful for humanity and likely to become more widespread. The Opposition considers that this surge of strong collective feeling is regional, if not national in character, and somewhat similar to that of the time of Tiradentes, when the people of Minas Gerais began to realize that one's motherland was, to a very great extent, the land in which one was born, and only to a much lesser extent the far-distant home of the sovereign. (*Ubi bene ibi patria*)

3. Although its patriotism is stronger than that of Dr Salazar and his followers, the Opposition refuses to believe that quiet and calm prevail in the Portuguese colonies because of the generosity of our colonial system. They prefer to attribute it to the lack of

politico-social culture and freedom of the native who is constantly kept under military control.

4. The Opposition recognizes the people's right to self-determination, with the logical and wise proviso that the exercise of this right is impossible if it does not coincide with the feelings and collective outlook of the the people, as opposed to those of tribes capable of rekindling fierce and primitive hatreds. To this end the Opposition recognizes and defends the need for urgent preparation of the people.

5. The Opposition does not take its stand with those who want to see chaos in the colonies.

6. The Opposition considers it criminal and anti-patriotic that a problem of such magnitude is not subject to the fullest national discussion, for the colonies are not the private property of Dr Salazar but form an integral part of the Portuguese nation, of which we, the Opposition, form the majority.

7. The Opposition believes that Dr Salazar's policy could lead the colonies into various dangers, including internecine conflicts, which must be prevented by methods other than military violence and police brutality. The Opposition does not forget the Nation's great historical past and accepts the responsibilities entailed. It is prepared to adopt new methods, while refusing the advice of those who treat several highly civilized white European nations like forcibly occupied colonies.

8. The Opposition does not consider that Africa is the sole property of the Negroes, but rather of all Africans, especially those who were born there. With due allowance for special circumstances, this principle applies to other colonies in any part of the world.

9. The Opposition, in its search for a solution, is equally opposed to the Communist system and the capitalist exploitation of the Negro.

10. The Opposition considers that the emancipation of the native is both humane and beneficial to the Nation, even from the economic and commercial

points of view, since his purchasing power would be increased.

Having established these ten points, we will now consider how they can be put into practice.

11. The Opposition aims to establish a Federal Republic of the United States of Portugal.

12. This Republic would be constituted by the federation of peoples under the protection of the Portuguese flag and would recognize their right to self-determination. It would also establish the legal definition of the word 'people'.

13. The Constitution of the Federal Republic will be approved by a plebiscite, as will the Constitution of each individual state.

14. The following federal states would be formed:
   —The Federal State, comprising Metropolitan Portugal, with its adjacent islands and those overseas governments of territories so small as to be unsuitable for the kind of statute applicable to the other colonies, i.e. São João Batista de Ajudá and Macau.
   —The State of Guinea (with the adjacent archipelago of Cape Verde)
   —The State of Angola (with the adjacent archipelãgo of São Tomé and Príncipe)
   —The State of Mozambique
   —The State of India (Goa, Damão and Diu)
   —The State of Timor.

15. As the numerical majority is at present far from corresponding to the proportional political reality, calculations would have to take this fact into account. The Opposition intends that the representation of Portuguese citizens still under a tribal régime shall be exercised by a representative vote through their chieftains.

16. The plebiscite would decide the following:
   a) Equality in the eyes of the law of the rights

of peoples and individuals, with no distinctions of race, colour, political or religious affinities. This equality of rights includes the distribution of political posts, which would be allotted only in regard to technical capacity.

b) The rights of representation of the citizens by direct or indirect vote.

c) The citizenship of those Portuguese under a tribal régime, taking into consideration traditional customs and usages and with the intention of establishing their civic rights and instituting measures to raise their social status.

d) The right to free elementary education and to higher grades of education for those who cannot meet the cost but show due qualifications. The declaration to found university colleges in the overseas territories in order to hasten the training of the native.

e) The right to social assistance.

f) The financial autonomy and self-government of the states.

g) The representation of the federal states in the Federal Government, including the political and administrative chambers.

h) The Federal State to have the right of decision in matters of federal policy, foreign policy, national defence, the supreme court of justice, economic co-ordination, political, administrative and social control.

i) The establishment of a time-limit for the government by a provisional régime between the proclamation of the federation of states, with the recognition of self-determination for the federal peoples, and the approval and coming into force of the Constitution of the Federal Republic.

I concluded this Colonial Plan of the Opposition with the following words:

'I have presented the carefully constructed plan of the Opposition, whose details were drawn up after consultation with various political and technical experts, both in Brazil and abroad. Fortunately, as Leader of the Opposition, I was in a good position to integrate these various opinions, being more than just an ordinary traveller. I have in fact paid visits in an official capacity to the Cape Verde Islands, São Tomé, Angola, Mozambique, Timor, Morocco, the French and Belgian Congos, the Union of South Africa, Bechuanaland, Kenya, Egypt, Burma, British India, and Dutch Timor, as well as to former British colonies now integrated into the Commonwealth, such as Australia, Canada, Newfoundland, and Trinidad. In my world tour I also had the opportunity of visiting the Pacific, where I saw Fiji and Hawaii.

'I consider that this historic declaration which the Opposition is making today is the finest act of homage that it could offer the Portuguese Republic on its fiftieth anniversary.

'Yet, sirs, as we give the press yet another piece of paper, let us not be blinded for, although all that we do enhances our prestige while detracting from that of the dictator, there is no substitute for the act of force essential to unseat him.

'Sirs, I fully intend that that day shall soon dawn. Let us look to the future and be glad! Long live Brazil! Long live Liberty! Long live the Republic!'

CHAPTER XVIII

The Beja revolt

In June and July 1961, I sent agents to Europe and Morocco to maintain contacts and put into action my plan for the revolution in Portugal.

I can give the general outline of this plan, since the next one is completely different and, anyhow, P.I.D.E. must have known about its predecessor for a long time. The main points were:

—Sudden attacks by a small number of men with imported arms upon one or more military units, situated in such a position that they might easily be cut off from the front and covered at the flanks and rear by extensive natural barriers. Thus we broke the manoeuvre down to the basic fact that A could only leave if B left and B only if A left.

—A swift raid, with increased numbers and the weapons taken during the earlier attacks, either upon neighbouring units or upon defensible positions which could be used to isolate completely the zone chosen as the stronghold of the revolution. The troops would find their own transport for this operation by requisitioning civilian vehicles.

—For communications and propaganda purposes, small training and tourist planes would be used, needing very little landing space and able to defend themselves when flying low.

—A mass insurrection in the secondary fields of operation, with assaults upon the small units of the National Republican Guard, the Fiscal Guard and the police force; in this way small nuclei would be formed which could regularly combine with larger groups to exercise punitive action upon the enemy and hinder their manoeuvres. The central authorities would also be overthrown at the same time.

Unfortunately this plan was changed, and the revolt broke out in the secondary field of operations, Alentejo. I was prevented from taking part in it by liaison difficulties with Morocco, my failure to meet a revolutionary agent, and also because I did not arrive in Portugal until shortly before the revolt started.

En route for Portugal

The general opinion was that I should not enter Portugal until a bridgehead had been established and although I disagreed it was not through any unwillingness on my part that I did not arrive earlier.

Unfortunately, apart from being extremely well known, I was provided with the so-called 'yellow' Brazilian passport for foreigners, which is the worst kind for getting through Spain. I had to wait from 4th October until 22nd December before I could finally leave with a Portuguese passport into which had been stuck a photograph of me in disguise, with glasses, moustache and cropped hair, and which had also been embossed with a forged white seal.

It was essential to pay minute attention to my suits and linen, to remove all marks of identification, my initials, tailors' labels, and anything else that might give rise to awkward or difficult questions should the P.I.D.E. search my luggage. I even had an engraved inscription erased from the bracelet of a watch which had been presented to me by some Brazilian friends.

To complicate matters, the passport I was using bore a stamp in Arabic which filled an entire page, and this stamp had not been filled in. This is not the place to explain why, for very good reasons. I was filled with apprehension, fearing that on crossing the Moroccan frontier I might be questioned because of it and fall into inconsistent statements, causing the police to suspect me. So might end, abruptly and ingloriously, a progress towards what I still seriously believed would be a war. On 23rd December 1961, I crossed the frontier of Ceuta, the Spanish enclave in Morocco.

As it was Christmas time, the line of cars passing slowly through the customs and police inspections was a long one. A friend sensibly put me in the company of three pretty Spanish girls, to travel in the car belonging to one of them. They did not know who I was, but had been told to get this gentleman, now ten years older in order to agree with the age given in the passport, and ailing, into Spain quickly, so that he could go and spend Christmas with his family in Portugal. . . .

I stayed in the car, pretending to be an ailing cripple, and they went to see to the passport. Actually the Moroccan police suspected something and became awkward, but in the end after much discussion in which I took no part *L'Eternel Féminin* got them to put the exit-stamp in my passport.

It is curious that at the very moment of my leaving a country that takes pleasure in the departure of foreigners, some kind of obstacle should arise.

Because of these delays I missed the boat that was to take me to Algeciras in Spain. The worst of it was that it was now Saturday, and there was no boat until Monday, which was Christmas Day.

My new-found young friends, very sad that I could not continue my journey, settled me in a modest hotel and took their leave. They were going to return straight away to Tetuán in Morocco.

Once again all the acting ability I had acquired, and that was little enough, began to fail me. It happened that in the hotel I filled in the registration form in a leisurely manner, in a very careful hand, such as would correspond with that of the owner of the passport. Yet suddenly, since for more than fifty years I had been one and the same person, Humberto Delgado, I forgot I was no longer that man, and signed the form with my usual signature—so different from that of the other person to be seen in the passport. Mine is illegible, but even so it did not bear the remotest resemblance to that of the owner of the passport. In a fraction of a second my subconscious reacted to an ultra-rapid nerve-message. I snatched the form from the hand of the clerk and tore it up carefully, putting the pieces in my pocket. I filled in another

What would the poor fellow think?

Dr Antonio de Oliveira Salazar (left). General Delgado (right)

A victim of a stray bullet is carried off to hospital on a stretcher during anti-government demonstrations in Lisbon, 1962

I went up to my room, trying to show the greatest calm. When I was certain that the maid was not going to come back, I undressed and relaxed.

Suddenly I heard voices and footsteps. There was a knock at my door. I went pale. Could it be anyone but the police? Who knew me in Ceuta by either of my identities, false or real? Moreover, the knock at the door was not that of a maid.

When I said 'Come in!', my voice sounded as if not of this world. ... I watched the door as if hypnotized. What would happen? Should I resist? What use would that be? Then the three Spanish girls came in, radiating cheerfulness, youth and feminine charm. They had decided to stay in Ceuta, and had come to see if I had settled in comfortably!

Having recovered from my fright, and being delighted to see them, I forgot that I was officially a cripple, and began to busy myself finding chairs for so many people.

I then noticed that one of them wore a look of amazement: 'So this is the gentleman they told us was so old and feeble?' I recovered myself and assumed my former pose again as best I could.

By the night of the 25th I was in Seville, where I spent four days trying to find horses and someone to smuggle me over the frontier so that I could avoid the frontier posts. I could not manage this and decided to head for Portugal in an ordinary bus on the morning of the 30th, for I guessed that the revolt which had been planned for the 3rd and which had still not occurred at Christmas would now have to be fixed for New Year's Day. I must mention here the part played by my courageous Brazilian secretary, D. Arajaryr Campos who, because funds were low, not only paid her own return air fare, but was also an excellent contact in Morocco, Spain and Portugal. Learning that I planned to cross the frontier alone, she determined that if I was shot or otherwise removed from the scene she would get the information through to the foreign news agencies. She bravely offered to accompany me, even taking charge of my uniform by hiding it in the lining of her coat and, as one of her real names was by coincidence the same as one of my assumed ones, we decided to pass ourselves off as uncle and niece in Spain and then cross over into Portugal.

Our entry into Portugal represented one of the worst moments, since the Portuguese passenger coach arrived fifty minutes later than the Spanish one, which made us spend all this time in agonizing doubt: Would I be discovered? Why did they not bring back the passport? From time to time the policemen chanced to look at the bus, but to us two 'criminals' it only seemed that each of these glances would be followed by their entering the vehicle to arrest us. At last I saw the passport. What a relief! Very soon after, the Portuguese bus arrived. We were informed that the Customs would dispense with opening our luggage. Why? Because it was near New Year's Eve? Because the torrential rain made them feel sorry for the passengers? I do not know, but I do know that it was an enormous weight off our shoulders. Inside a large coat belonging to Senhora Campos was my uniform.

But it was when we had to get out of the bus and walk fifty yards close to the Portuguese police that the worst phase of it all came. Senhora Campos, true to her role, lovingly helped her good 'uncle' to walk, and in this manner we passed by those wretched snoopers and got into the Portuguese bus. It was about 11 a.m.

I was now going to cross Portugal in broad daylight—I, who for a whole month had had my photograph in the newspapers, in leaflets and even on the walls, where Salazarist hatred had not torn it down during the electoral campaign of 1958.

Let us be frank. I was cold, but I was perspiring freely.

March on Beja

I crossed the frontier at Vila Nova de Ficalho, reaching Lisbon at dusk on 30th December, where I booked in at the Pensão São Jorge. The same night I contacted a former colleague in the revolution, but unfortunately he had not been told the entire plan and so I did not learn the exact position until 10 p.m. of the following day, some hours after the revolutionaries had left for Beja. I set out immediately and arrived there at two in the morning on 1st January, but was very taken aback to find everything completely quiet. It was not until we drove around trying to find the barracks that the police, who had remained quiet up to then, suddenly and very peremptorily ordered the car to stop. The driver hesitated but then, giving the appropriate signal, drove slowly on without stopping, and the police, who were also dubious, did not fire. When we turned the next corner, we shot forward as fast as possible and went to the hideout where I had been asked in Lisbon to await the result of the first part of the operation, the capture of the garrison. When this was over, we had planned to form columns of cars to attack the south, but everything went wrong. As commander-in-chief I would be in charge of the columns and make an announcement to the country over the radio as president of the J.N.L.I. (National Independent Committee for the Liberation), whose members would immediately be chosen, on a provisional basis, from whoever was available.

Candidly, the troops stationed outside Beja were not neutralized and a short while later we heard over the radio in our hideout that the whole thing had been put down in a few hours. Meanwhile the owner of the house had made his family leave. It was agreed that whenever he was out of the house it should be supposed that it was empty. Imagine the effort and discipline necessary in such a tiny place, where only one copy of one newspaper arrived each day. What misery! We could not have a light except in the kitchen. Every time there was a knock at the door, we stood stock still. The caller would persist, and our hearts only beat normally when we saw that the caller had given up.

Dona Arajaryr (or Senhora Campos as she is more properly and better known) cooked for us. I stood watching her bent over a fireplace level with the ground, something she had never seen before, using a fan to kindle the fire, a thing she had never used in Brazil, for wood and charcoal fires are only used by the poor! Later, the three of us—she, the revolutionary who had come with us from Lisbon (I had sent the chauffeur back to Lisbon at once, so that in the village they would not even see the registration number of the car) and myself—and at times also the owner of the house—sitting at the kitchen table or by the hearth, would savour the refreshment she had prepared. We ate slowly, for this was a way of helping to pass the time, which seemed so long, so gloomy, and dominated always by constant nervous tension.

The actual revolt

I have already said that the plan was changed but as everyone was either taken prisoner or killed I could not get into contact with the leaders in order to find out the reason. I think that the strength of the new plan and the reason for the change lay in the different choice of locality, since some officers of the 3rd Infantry Regiment stationed in Beja were in the plot and could arrange for the revolutionaries to enter the garrison without any preliminary fighting. Thus it was completely wrong for the papers to say that a 'fortress' had been 'attacked', because there was no fortress and no attack. Even more erroneous was the rumour that I, a general, would be manning a machine-gun at the head of the brave men in Captain Varela Gomes's platoon; a captain was quite sufficient for so few troops.

At dawn on the 1st, the Army Minister published an official bulletin: 'Subversive elements attacked the garrison of the 3rd Infantry Regiment in Beja and very soon managed to gain entrance to the soldiers' quarters.' He gave the names of the units which had fought against the rebels and announced that Captain Varela Gomes, the leader of the civilians, had been wounded, and that the Under-Secretary of State for the Army, Lieutenant-Colonel Jaime Felipe de Fonseca, had gone to Beja 'in order to see at close quarters what measures had been taken to restore order.'

At 1 p.m. another bulletin was issued announcing that the Under-Secretary 'had died, wounded by the bullets of the same traitors who at dawn this morning attempted to capture the garrison of the 3rd Infantry Regiment at Beja'.

A last communiqué finally gave details, describing how two officers of the unit, Captain Vasconcelos Pestana and Lieutenant Hipólito dos Santos, had entered the garrison unopposed and followed by another vehicle, which was seen by the officer on duty, Second Lieutenant Arantes e Oliveira, who was immediately handcuffed.

'With the officer on duty out of action, and having free

access to the garrison, some of the attackers, including Captain Varela Gomes, proceeded to the room of Major Calapez Martins, the second in command who, when woken up by violent bangings on his door, realized that something unusual was in progress. Half opening the door, he recognized Captain Varela Gomes and, as they struggled, he wounded him with a shot from his revolver. After this, Major Calapez Martins tried to alert and summon the local Social Security Police and National Republican Guard who had already been warned by some of the local inhabitants.'

The revolt was over before daybreak. Inevitably, the report ended in the usual way: 'It would seem from information already obtained and evidence from those involved in this attempted sedition, that it was planned and carried out by the Communist Party.'

'. . . After the necessary inquiries, the Minister for the Army has decided that, in view of the seriousness of the crime, the following officers will be dismissed with ignominy as being unfit to wear the same uniform as their compatriots who are fighting for their country in our overseas provinces.' A list of five names was given and then the bulletin went on to say that, following the usual custom, this punishment, which would be put into effect immediately, was independent of the normal legal procedure that would follow.

The number of civilians who took part was thought to be about thirty, which really was not very many. Yet the most caustic critics are either foreigners, who have not the slightest idea of what it is like to live under the Salazarist régime, to be interrogated and tortured by P.I.D.E. and see one's family ruined, or else the so-called Portuguese members of the Opposition, who cause more harm to their party than many supporters of Salazar and even P.I.D.E. itself.

The aftermath

After two days in the hideout in Beja, I headed for Oporto in the north, where I arrived after a good nine hours of night driving, having been stopped three times by military officials and road patrols, who fortunately did not recognize me. On my arrival in Oporto, I booked in for one night at the Pensão

Aviz, and for the benefit of any doubting Thomases, let me add that I stayed in room 21 and Senhora Campos in room 1. The owner of the pension will confirm this and keep it in mind for use in any future history of illegal entries into Portugal. On account of the strict check on the main roads and frontiers, several of my colleagues wanted me to seek asylum again in the Brazilian Embassy, but I would not agree. I even tried to see my family, whom I had telephoned under a false name in Lisbon just before I left for Beja, but this was impossible. When I learnt that I would not be able to avoid the police post at Chaves and cross the frontier there because of the strict watch being kept, I set out on 10th January 1962 for Barca d'Alva. (There was a rumour in Oporto that I was in the city disguised as a fishwife!) In Barca d'Alva I was forced to spend the night in the miserable Restaurante-Pensão at the station, sleeping right over the P.I.D.E. post! On the 11th I crossed the frontier en route for Fregenada and Salamanca, Medina del Campo and Madrid. In order to throw any hounds off the scent, Senhora Campos had crossed by the Beira Alta line at Vilar Formoso.

The journey towards Spain, in order to go on to Brazil via Morocco, filled me with the greatest apprehension. I was the only first-class passenger as the big floods on the River Douro had wrecked or blocked 70 kilometres of railway track. For this reason hardly anyone was leaving for the frontier at that point. I believed there was only one other passenger and he was travelling third-class. I had to get out at Pinhão, change to a bus which took me to Ferradosa and take the train there again for Barca d'Alva, a very small village, one of the greatest amusements of whose officials is to watch the train arrive at the tiny railway station.

Standing on the steps of the carriage ready to get off, I saw about eight people, all officials, casting their eyes over the passengers. The phenomena of perspiration and so on began again.

But, 'believe it or not', as Ripley would say, as I was about to set foot on the station platform, there was a general electrical break-down which plunged everything into darkness. Mystical natures might attribute it to a miracle.

I did not wait to find out if I was officially a cripple here. I made a sudden sprint for the miserable hotel-restaurant that functions over the station, and ran up the steps two at a time to the first floor. With bursting lungs (the cases were heavy) I blurted out: 'I cannot climb stairs. I want a room and will have all my meals there.' (The restaurant was on the ground floor). By a freak of fate the hotel, which has only six rooms, had one free—room number 6, to be precise. I did not leave it until I caught the train next day, for there was no connection for Spain until then.

I was then confronted with the next serious problem: to present myself next day in person in the P.I.D.E. office to get the exit stamp. It was a lot to ask of a man who, through an unbroken run of good luck and the stupidity of the police, was still at liberty.

One of my three pairs of glasses had lenses a little larger than is usual. These served to press down the lower lids while I let the upper lids droop. When the policeman, six-footer though he was, saw this fantastic fabrication of a human being that I was, with frighteningly Frankenstein eyes, he at once told me to go to the train where I would be given my passport. I sat down, wrapped myself up in my overcoat, drew my scarf up to my nose and my hat down to my eyebrows. When I was given my passport, my face could hardly be seen.

Counting the day of my departure, I spent thirteen days in Portugal and stayed at eight different places: three pensions and five private houses, four of which were in the north.

Early on the morning of the 12th, I arrived in Madrid, where I stayed only six hours to obtain a visa for Morocco, and at six o'clock on the same day I was in Casablanca. Between the airport and my hotel I completely changed my identity, for I was no longer Sr X but once more General Humberto Delgado who officially had never left Morocco. I switched back to my Brazilian passport and changed the labels on my cases so that it would not look as though I was carrying stolen luggage. I went to a hotel where I had never stayed before, announcing that I had just arrived from Rabat, the capital. On 16th January I re-entered Brazil quietly and unadvertised.

Some people, who were already becoming sceptical of the

Opposition after Galvão's claim to have entered Portugal, seemed to think that this was only another bluff. Fortunately, however, among the seven stamps on my passport, two are those of the P.I.D.E. confirming my entry on 30th December 1961 and departure on 11th January 1962.

Since it did not become known until some two weeks later that I was in Beja on the actual night of the revolt, the press did not give much publicity to the fact. Nevertheless, the National Broadcasting Company of New York commissioned its Moroccan representative, John Cooley, to make a film about it and also various newspapers referred to the affair, for example the *Christian Science Monitor*, *Time*, *The Guardian*, *Le Mond*, the *Daily Mail*, not to mention almost all the important Brazilian dailies, in particular *A Folha de São Paulo*, the *Diário de Notícias*, the *Jornal de Brazil*, *Manchete*, *Ultima Hora*, *Malhete* and the Moroccan papers. Among the papers of the Portuguese Opposition, the homage which the *Lusitano do Rio* paid to the brave men under Captain Varela Gomes is especially memorable. Here are some extracts:

'. . . Aware of the gravity and nobility of their mission, the handful of brave men boldly confronted the danger. . . . To judge by results, their heroic action failed, but in fact it triumphed, for it has proved just what the Portuguese Opposition can do when organized and ably commanded by someone whose combination of intelligence, strategic ingenuity and courage is without precedent in the history of the Portuguese Opposition.

'Your Excellency General Humberto Delgado, Leader of the Opposition; António Pedro Correia Vila, killed in battle; David da Silva Abreu, killed in battle; the heroic Captain João Maria Paulo Varela Gomes, seriously wounded and taken prisoner; Captain Eugénio Oscar Felipe de Oliveira, taken prisoner; Captain Francisco António de Vasconcelos Pestana, taken prisoner; Lt. Jorge Manuel Toscana de Melo, taken prisoner; Dr António Francisco Correia da Graça Miranda, taken prisoner; Gualter Viriato Nunes Basílio, taken prisoner; Manuel Serra and his companions, all taken prisoner; and all other participants in the revolt.

'Your country will never forget you and will be grateful to you for ever.

'O Lusitano.'

The consequences of the revolution and my journey

Although this is of secondary importance, I must point out that my adventure was not only a blow to the prestige of Salazar's and Franco's police, but also proved the incompetence of their staff. Yet no doubt we must make allowances, for they could not have imagined that I should have the audacity to pass in disguise through the frontier posts, for they all thought that I would try to cross at one of the unguarded stretches which are only subject to periodic check-ups.

It also gave a tremendous psychological lift to the Portuguese people by increasing their faith in a leader who had promised, as the photograph of the passport stamps I had distributed shows, that he would return—and did return! In this way I managed to reinstate an Opposition which had been scoffed at both inside and outside the country, because of the farcical antics of the clique I have mentioned earlier.

I should like to point out that from the point of view of the revolution this rebellion represented the end of planning and the symbolic opening of direct action. It is perfectly true that since 26th August 1931 the Opposition had not fired a single shot and I do not believe that one newspaper in the world was aware of this until I drew attention to it.

Beja was symbolically important in another way, for it showed a new alliance between the officers of the regular army, the reserves and members of the long-suffering masses. The *ancien régime* type of Portuguese, wistfully dreaming of a Republic similar to that of 1910, and the pampered sons of the gentry who have also come to believe in this vague, obsolete ideal, a merely political, rather than an undisguisedly politico-economic and progressive Republic, were not among those who fought at Beja. It is auspicious that the new generation considers government from the point of view of economics in the twentieth century manner, not in the garrulous fashion of the previous century.

I should like to emphasize that as far as we can see the

Portuguese Communist party has changed its attitude and at last arrived at the conclusion that the dictatorship will not be overthrown by elections, but with guns and violence.

It is worth mentioning also that my journey and the revolt proved the effectiveness of the Luso-Spanish agreement which I signed on 26th November 1960, as I have already stated in an earlier chapter. Through the exiled Spanish Government and their representative in São Paulo, Commander Lorenzo Serrano, who played an important part in the rebellion, I and my agents in Europe and Africa were given excellent facilities.

Expulsion from Brazil?

On my return to Brazil I was faced with the risk of expulsion because, according to press reports, I had avowed responsibility for the Portuguese revolt and so, when brought before the Director-General of Justice, Dr Dardeau de Carvalho, I confirmed my responsibility without giving him time to read the collection of newspaper cuttings which he wanted me to hear. I then stated that I refused to abstain from further conspiracies with my contacts throughout the world for, by making such a concession, I should be betraying my principles as Leader of the Opposition. This put the Brazilian Government into an intriguing dilemma, for if they expelled me and no other country was prepared to give me asylum, I would be handed over to P.I.D.E. who would either kill or imprison me, but if they did not expel me, the Portuguese Government would be even more discountenanced. Between the devil and the deep, blue sea. . . . Even as I finish these memoirs, I still do not know their decision.

When we start to make new plans for a rebellion, it will be extremely encouraging to remember that the Spaniards in Morocco called the Beja revolt the *Jaca Portuguesa*—Portuguese Pony—and thus compared it to the small, immediately suppressed revolt which heralded the setting up of the Spanish Republic. Is this a good omen? I am not superstitious but, as the Spaniards say, 'I don't believe in witches, but I am sure there are such things'.

Some thirty people spoke to me while I was in Portugal,

that is to say, thirty who knew who I really was, and no doubt, in spite of the danger involved, they were unable to resist the temptation to tell others that they had 'touched the hand of the saint', because it is a well-known psychological fact that a person is respected according to how much more he knows or possesses than his neighbour. This is particularly true of Portugal where, three centuries after King Sebastian had been killed in the Battle of Alcacer Quibir (Morocco), the people still believed that this poor, mad young man would return to save their country, even though he would have been as old as Methuselah. Add to this their innate tendency for the mysterious, the rumours spread around about my brief stay in the north of Portugal, the announcements by foreign radio stations and in the odd foreign newspaper that found its way in, and the distribution over the years of the stamps bearing my portrait and the motto: 'I shall return', and you will understand the special excitement in the air, which kindled the very hearts and souls of the people who had sought their salvation in the elections of 1958.

It is not therefore surprising that only a month after the Beja revolt and twenty days after my stay in the north, a message from the international news agencies reported disturbances in Oporto: 'Salazar's security police broke up a political demonstration in Oporto tonight by firing on a crowd of some 5,000 people. At least eighteen were wounded and it is not known whether any were killed. As well as firing on the crowd, the police turned hoses upon the demonstrators, who scattered with shouts of 'Liberty' and 'Long live General Delgado'. Since the presidential election of 1958, this city, traditionally the centre of Portuguese political disturbances, has remained peaceful, but we remember that it was on 31st January seventy-one years ago that the unsuccessful rebellion against the monarchy took place.'

On 26th March, the students of Lisbon University went on strike because they had been refused permission to celebrate their annual festival. This demonstration reminded me of the mutual affection between the younger generation and myself during the electoral campaign. Dr Salazar believes that the younger generation is largely becoming Communist. The

Armed Forces and other reactionary classes do not face Communism in the same way as the great democracies, but continue to take the blackest view of it.

The Armed Forces and other stupid reactionary classes should, however, realize that the *longer Dr Salazar remains in power the more Communists there will be.* I say this not because I am a Communist myself, but because I have not let my brain be numbed by the thirty-three years of Dr Salazar's reign. Modern in outlook as I am, and having spent so many years abroad among Anglo-Saxons, I am too broadminded and tolerant to be afraid of these 'isms'.

The country must be governed by the younger generation between twenty-one and fifty, the so-called 'third force'. It is with deep emotion and affection that I exhort them to continue their demonstrations and become ever stronger, braver and more confident of their Cause, for only in this way will they spur the country on towards the national rebellion which must finally liberate our struggling people.

INDEX

225